Benson

THE BIBLE STORY

for Boys and Girls

NEW TESTAMENT

WALTER RUSSELL BOWIE

NEW YORK • NASHVILLE

Abingdon Press

To Davy and Judy
and Joanie and Scotty
in token that they may
"continue Christ's faithful soldiers
and servants unto their life's end."

The Contents

Color Plates

Black-and-white illustrations by Stephani and Edward Godwin

THE BIBLE STORY FOR BOYS AND GIRLS

New Testament

CHAPTER ONE

The Baby Jesus

A long time ago the greatest city in the world was the city of Rome. The Roman armies had marched far and won many battles. Augustus Caesar was the emperor of Rome and of all the lands that the Roman soldiers had conquered. When Augustus spoke, men near and far had to listen and follow his commands.

Yet, almost two thousand years later, it is not Augustus Caesar whom people remember, but a baby who was born when Augustus ruled the Roman world. That baby, Jesus, was more important than Augustus and all the other emperors and kings. He was more important than anyone else who has lived before or since.

The part of the Bible which we call the New Testament tells the story of Jesus. It tells how he was born, what he was like, how he lived and what he did, and what others did because of him.

The first four books in the New Testament are called the Gospels—the Gospel of Matthew, the Gospel of Mark, the Gospel of Luke, and the Gospel of John. The Gospel of Mark was written first and is the shortest. The Gospel of John was written last.

The books which tell of Jesus' birth are the Gospel of Matthew and the Gospel of Luke. The writers of these books were not there when Jesus was born. So when they began to write they gathered together the beautiful stories which were being told by those who said they knew what had happened.

The first story, in the Gospel of Luke, is about a boy who was born a little while before Jesus.

In Jerusalem there was a priest named Zacharias. He was an old man. His wife, whose name was Elisabeth, was old too. Zacharias and Elisabeth did not have any children. But one day when Zacharias was in the Temple a wonderful thing happened. He had just put some sweet-smelling incense into the flame that was burning on the altar. Suddenly in the midst of the smoke he saw an angel, and he was afraid. He heard the angel say, "Zacharias, do not be afraid." The angel told him that God had listened to his prayers, and that his wife, Elisabeth, would have a son. The angel said they should name the baby John, and that when this baby grew up God would use him to be a messenger to tell the people of glorious things that were to come.

Zacharias could hardly believe that what he heard was true. But the angel spoke again. "I am Gabriel," he said, "and I stand in the presence of God. He sent me to speak to you, and to bring you this good news."

At that, Zacharias became speechless. When he went out into another part of the Temple, where some people were gathered to pray, he could not say a word to them. All that he could do was to make signs. By these signs the people understood that Zacharias had seen a vision. Then Zacharias went home and he wrote down for Elisabeth what he had heard the angel tell.

Elisabeth had a cousin, Mary, who lived in the little town of Nazareth. She was young and lovely. She was happy, too, because she was engaged to be married to Joseph, the carpenter. One day Gabriel, the same angel who had come to Zacharias, came to Mary. He was all splendid with the light of God. When Mary looked up she saw the glorious angel, and she heard him speak. At first she was afraid, just as Zacharias had been. But the angel said to her, "Fear not, Mary, for you have found favor with God."

Then Gabriel told her that she was going to have a baby.

"He will be great, and will be called the Son of the Most High," said Gabriel. "And the Lord God will give to him the throne of . . . David, . . . and of his kingdom there will be no end."

"How can this be?" Mary, hushed and wondering, asked the angel. The angel told her that God's spirit would come upon her. The child to be born, the angel said, should be called "the Son of God." The angel told Mary that her cousin Elisabeth was soon to have a son, too.

Mary said to the angel, "Let it be with me according to your word." When she looked up, the angel was gone.

Mary arose and started out with eager haste toward the hills of Judea, where Elisabeth and Zacharias lived. When she came

to Elisabeth's house, Elisabeth gave a cry of joy. And Mary sang
for her a hymn which we call the Magnificat. It came straight
from her heart and praised God just as he had been praised so
often in the psalms she knew.

This is the way her song began:

"My soul doth magnify the Lord,
    And my spirit hath rejoiced in God . . ."

After Mary had finished her visit with Elisabeth, she went
back to Nazareth. Not long afterward, Elisabeth's baby was born.

When the baby was eight days old, Elisabeth and Zacharias took
him up to the Temple in Jerusalem. It was the custom for all
Jewish fathers and mothers to take their babies there to ask God
to bless them. The relatives and friends who came with Zacharias
and Elisabeth thought that the baby would be named after his
father. They were surprised when Elisabeth said, "He must be
called John."

They turned to the baby's father. Zacharias still could not say
a word. He asked for something on which to write, and he wrote,
"His name is John." Then, of a sudden, Zacharias' voice came
back to him and he could speak. Loudly and clearly he praised
God. And, full of joy, he began to sing:

"Blessed be the Lord God of Israel,
For he has visited and redeemed his people . . .

"And thou, child, shalt be called the prophet of the Most High;
For thou shalt go before the Lord to prepare his ways; . . .

"To give light to those who sit in darkness . . .
To guide our feet into the way of peace."

After Mary came back from her visit to Elisabeth, she stayed
in Nazareth with Joseph, to whom she had been married. As

Gabriel the angel had promised, she was to nave a baby, but her baby was not born in Nazareth.

Augustus Caesar, the emperor of Rome, had commanded that a new tax should be collected from all the people over whom he ruled. Everyone had to pay the tax money at the place where his family had lived and where his name was written on the list for taxing.

Now Joseph, according to the Gospel of Luke, belonged to a family that was descended from David, the great king. The home of the family of David had been Bethlehem, so Joseph had to go there to pay his tax. He did not want to leave Mary behind in Nazareth, so he took her with him.

Bethlehem was many miles from Nazareth, and there was no easy way to go. Joseph put Mary on a donkey. But he had to walk by her side, and so they were a long time on the road. Mary was very tired when she came to the journey's end. She and Joseph hoped they could find a place to stay in Bethlehem. But the town was filled with people who had come earlier, and there was no room for Mary and Joseph at the inn. All they could find was a little space in a stable. There, that night, with only the sleepy cattle standing near, Mary's baby was born — the baby Jesus. The Gospel of Luke tells that when the baby Jesus was born his mother wrapped him in swaddling cloths and laid him in a manger.

At first hardly anyone knew that the coming of this baby would make a difference to the world. Augustus Caesar, the emperor, in his rich palace in far-off Rome, heard nothing of it. If someone had told him, he would not have cared. What did it matter to him that a baby had been born in a small town in distant Palestine? He would have thought that no baby born in a stable could amount to much. He did not know what would be written about that baby in the Gospel of Luke.

This is what the Gospel tells:

"And in that region there were shepherds out in the field, keeping watch over their flock by night. And an angel of the Lord appeared to them, and the glory of the Lord shone around them, and they were filled with fear. And the angel said to them, 'Be not afraid; for behold, I bring you good news of a great joy which will come to all the people; for to you is born this day in the city of David a Savior, who is Christ the Lord. And this will be a sign for you: you will find a babe wrapped in swaddling cloths and lying in a manger.'

"And suddenly there was with the angel a multitude of the heavenly host praising God and saying,

" 'Glory to God in the highest,
and on earth peace among men
with whom he is pleased!'

"When the angels went away from them into heaven, the shepherds said to one another, 'Let us go over to Bethlehem and see this thing that has happened, which the Lord has made known to us.' And they went with haste, and found Mary and Joseph, and the babe lying in a manger. And when they saw it they made known the saying which had been told them concerning this child:

"And all who heard it wondered at what the shepherds told them. But Mary kept all these things, pondering them in her heart. And the shepherds returned, glorifying and praising God for all they had heard and seen, as it had been told them."

At the time when Jesus was born, Herod was the king whom the Romans allowed to rule over the part of Palestine called

Benson

THE BABY JESUS

Becher

JESUS IN THE CARPENTER SHOP

Judea. Jerusalem was in Judea and so was Bethlehem. Herod was a cruel old man. When he thought people were his enemies, he had them killed. The older he grew, the more he suspected everyone who seemed to be in his way. He was king in his own little place, and he hated the thought that anyone else might come to be king instead of him.

In a country far off to the east, the Gospel of Matthew tells us, there were wise men who studied the stars. They believed that they could tell from the stars when great things might happen on the earth. One night they saw in the sky a new star. They had heard an old, old saying which had been told among the Jewish people who had been captives there in the East:

"There shall come forth a star out of Jacob,
And a scepter shall rise out of Israel.'

Perhaps the wise men thought this meant that the new star in the sky was a sign that a great new king was coming among the people of Israel. They decided to find out.

So they set out on a journey in the direction pointed by the star. Across long miles of desert they rode on their camels. They went past the great city of Damascus, down the valleys, across the plains, and over the hills until they came to Jerusalem. There they stopped at the palace of Herod. They entered and stood before him.

"Where is he who has been born King of the Jews?" they asked. "For we have seen his star in the East, and have come to worship him."

"King of the Jews!" Who was King of the Jews but Herod? And what talk was this of someone else born to be king? That was what Herod asked himself. He was very angry, but he was too crafty to let the wise men see how angry he was. He looked at them as though he were very much interested in the news they had brought. He called together some of the priests and others who knew all the old writings. He asked them whether they had read anything about where a new king was to be born.

These learned men remembered and told what had been written a long time before by the prophet Micah. Micah was looking forward to the coming of the Messiah, the one whom he believed God would send to be the Savior of the people of Israel. Micah had said that the Messiah would come out of Bethlehem.

When the wise men heard this they were glad. They thought they knew now where they could find the king for whom they were looking. So they left the court of Herod in Jerusalem and took the road that led to the little town of Bethlehem.

The Gospel of Matthew does not say how many wise men there were, but the stories told about them, since long ago, say there were three, and that they were very rich. The story in Matthew says that the wise men followed their star until it stopped above the stable in Bethlehem. There they found Mary and Joseph and the little child Jesus. They bowed down before him. Then they opened their treasures and offered him the gifts they had brought — gold, and frankincense, and myrrh, a rare perfume.

Herod had commanded the wise men to let him know if they found the young child for whom they were looking. "Come back and tell me," he said, "and I will go and worship him too." But the wise men did not trust Herod. They had a dream about him, warning them not to go back to tell him. So they went home to their own country by another way.

When Herod learned that the wise men had gone home without coming back to him, he was furious. He was afraid that some child who had been born in Bethlehem might grow up to be king. So the Gospel of Matthew says that Herod sent his soldiers to Bethlehem, with orders to kill every young boy child there.

But it tells too that Joseph had been warned in a dream and that he and Mary with the child Jesus had fled into Egypt, where they hid until they heard that Herod was dead. Then they went back to their own home in Nazareth.

But before they had fled from Bethlehem, Joseph and Mary had taken the baby Jesus to the Temple in Jerusalem to be blessed. When Mary and Joseph came in, a good old man named Simeon saw them. All his life he had thought a great deal about God and had prayed to him. Simeon believed that some day he would see with his own eyes the one whom God would send to be the Messiah for whom all the people of Israel had been longing. Simeon took the child Jesus into his arms. He said that now he could die in peace because he had seen the one who had been waited for so long. This child, he said, would grow up to be like a great light, to show the way not only to his own people of Israel but to other peoples also.

CHAPTER TWO

The Boy of Nazareth

Joseph and Mary brought Jesus back to Nazareth. Soon he grew big enough to go and come by himself.

Nazareth was a village in the hills. The people lived in small, plain houses. On the doorpost of every house there was a tiny case in which there were words, copied from the sacred writings, which told of God:

"Hear, O Israel: The Lord our God is one Lord: and thou shalt love the Lord thy God with all thy heart, and with all thy soul, and with all thy might."

Whenever anyone went in or out of the door, he would touch

the little case that held the written words, and so he would be helped to remember what they said. When Jesus was old enough to understand, Mary told him what she knew of God, and she sang to him the psalms which told of God's love and of men's trust in God. Joseph told Jesus stories of the Jewish heroes who had lived long ago and taught him how God had helped men to understand and to live right since the time of Abraham. Every time the family came together for a meal, each person would fold his hands, and Joseph would thank God for their food. He would say: "Blessed art thou, O Lord our God, King of the Universe, who bringest forth bread from the earth."

In Nazareth there was a synagogue. There the people went on the Sabbath Day to hear the sacred books read and to say their prayers. When they came home on the Sabbath evening, they lighted a lamp and, as the children stood in the glow of it, the father blessed each one.

One of the great celebrations of the year was the Feast of Lights, a festival to remind the people of the time when the Temple at Jerusalem had been cleansed and made beautiful again after it had been in the hands of heathen people. At the time of this Feast of Lights, new lights were lighted every night for a week — as many lights as there were children in the home. By the last evening the whole house was bright, and everyone was reminded that God gives his light more and more to those who want to learn from him the way they ought to live.

Besides learning of God, Jesus learned about people. Little brothers and sisters came into the family, and Jesus helped Mary take care of them. He walked with his mother to the well to draw water. He watched her as she kneaded leaven into the dough and made the bread. In his carpenter shop close by, Joseph made wooden yokes for oxen, and plows, and beams for houses. Jesus watched him and learned to work with him. Jesus knew the people who came to the shop, and he saw what went on in the town and in the fields around it. He walked beside men who were sowing seed on plowed ground in the spring; he followed the men who reaped the harvest in the fall; he helped the shepherds to bring the flocks home in the evening, or went to look for a lamb that had been lost.

As he grew older Jesus went farther from Nazareth and he saw more. He went back and forth on the roads on the other side of the Nazareth hills, and to the larger cities on the shore of the Lake of Galilee, half a day's walk away. Sometimes he met a caravan of merchants, with the dusty camels laden with goods brought from far-off countries. Sometimes he met a company of Roman soldiers marching somewhere and making people stand off the road as they went by. He saw their hard faces and he saw people look at them with hatred and with fear.

Before Jesus was born, some men of Galilee had formed a Jewish army, under a leader named Judas. They had captured the city of Sepphoris, not far from Nazareth. These Jewish soldiers thought that they might start a war against the Romans. They hoped this war would spread so far that it would drive the Romans out of the whole country of Palestine. But a Roman army came and laid siege to Sepphoris. They broke down its gates and fought their way into its streets. They drove back the men who were defending the city, and they set fire to it. The men of Galilee who were not killed in the fighting were taken and hung up on crosses which the Romans set up along the roads.

Jesus had heard this story often and he understood why most of the Jewish people hated the Romans.

But why must the world be like that? he wondered. The Romans had made war against many countries. Now many of the peoples in these countries wanted more than anything else to kill their conquerors. In a family, people did not behave that way.

In a home where there was a father who loved his children and taught them to love one another, they did not hate and fight and kill. Instead, they tried to see how helpful to one another they could be.

Suppose all the people in the world could think of themselves as one great family? Suppose they could remember that that is exactly what they really are? All the people on the earth, Jesus knew, have one heavenly Father, God. Since all are his children, they should behave like brothers. It was not important that the Romans should go on conquering more kingdoms and all the while making more people hate them. It was not important, either, that the Jewish people should try to drive the Romans out and set up a kingdom of their own.

There was only one thing that Jesus thought important. That was that all men everywhere should know that they are brothers in one family and should begin to live as brothers ought to live. People would no longer be making war against one another. There would be one kingdom, and that would be the kingdom of God. Then there would be peace and happiness everywhere.

Perhaps there was hardly anyone in Nazareth who knew what Jesus was thinking. Mostly they were content with the same ideas, and with doing the same things in the same way they had done before. But the older Jesus grew, the more he thought about God, and the more he wanted to help everybody understand what it would mean to have God's kingdom come on earth.

When Jesus was twelve years old, he went with Joseph and Mary to Jerusalem to celebrate the Feast of the Passover. This was the greatest festival of the Jewish year. It had begun far back in the time of Moses, when the people of Israel were slaves

in the land of Egypt. They had worked there making bricks for
the temples and for the great monuments which Pharaoh, king
of Egypt, commanded to be built. The story of all that happened
then is written in the Old Testament Book of Exodus. The Feast
of the Passover was the glad reminder of the way in which Moses
helped the people of Israel to escape from Egypt and led them
across the Red Sea to Palestine, the Promised Land. Everyone was
happy when this festival came. It made men proud to remember
God's help long ago, and it filled them with belief that God was
with them still.

Jewish families always wanted to celebrate the Passover in
Jerusalem, where the Temple was. Thousands and thousands of
people, beyond anybody's counting, went up to the Holy City at
Passover time. All of them were happy at the thought that they
were going to see Jerusalem, the Holy City. They sang the beautiful old songs called the "pilgrim songs," which had first been
written hundreds of years before.

One of them began:

"I was glad when they said unto me,
  Let us go into the house of the Lord.
  Our feet shall stand within thy gates, O Jerusalem."

And another song began:

"As the mountains are round about Jerusalem,
  So the Lord is round about his people
    from henceforth even for ever."

Hardly anything could have been so exciting to Jesus as this
first journey to Jerusalem. Joseph's family and their friends
walked together in the midst of the growing crowds. The neighbors went too, and people from other towns along the way joined
them. They stopped now and then by the roadside to eat the

food they had brought with them. It was much more than one day's journey from Nazareth to Jerusalem. So at night they made a place to sleep on the ground and lay down under the open skies and the stars.

The Passover was in the spring, when the fruit trees were blossoming and the fields were bright with flowers. The road from Nazareth to Jerusalem led across the wide Plain of Esdraelon. Jesus knew the stories of the heroes who had walked on that same ground. Gideon had been there with his three hundred men; and David, and Jonathan, and Saul. Many armies had marched across it. Here and there in the earth one might come upon a broken sword blade or a piece of rusty iron from a chariot that had lain there for hundreds of years, left from some battle with the Philistines or the Egyptians or the terrible armies of the Assyrians.

After the pilgrims to Jerusalem had crossed the Plain of Esdraelon, they did not keep straight on. Instead, they crossed the Jordan River and went through the country on the east side of the river. Jesus knew that this was because the people of Israel despised the Samaritans, who lived in the country just beyond the Plain of Esdraelon, and did not want to go into the Samaritans' land.

Along the valley of the Jordan River the roads ran south as far as the fords opposite the old city of Jericho. Here the travelers went back across the river. Then they began to climb up through the steep hills that led toward Jerusalem. Up and up they went, until at last they came to where they could see the Holy City. The first sight of it made them stand still in happy wonder.

Outside the walls of Jerusalem, and also within the walls, were green gardens that belonged to rich men's houses. On the highest hill was the splendid palace which Herod the king had built. A great tower of it rose against the sky. But the most glorious thing was the Temple. It was even more magnificent than the Temple of Solomon which had stood on the same ground long before. The walls and columns were of colored marble, and great gates opened from each court to the court beyond. At the end of the farthest court there stood the holiest part of the Temple, so beautiful that hardly any other building in the world could be compared to it. Its marble walls were richly carved, and its roof was of shining gold.

Now that Joseph and Mary and Jesus had reached Jerusalem, they made ready for the Passover. Each family ate the Passover supper by itself. As the evening grew dark, a lamp was lighted, and the old, old prayers were said. Then the family ate a roasted lamb, and bread that had no yeast in it. They ate with their belts tightened and their sandals tied, because they were remembering the night when Moses had told the Hebrew people to be ready to leave Egypt the instant he should give the word. The people of Israel were no longer in Egypt, but again they were not free. Rome ruled over them. Roman soldiers were there in the castle on the hill, next to the Temple. Many men who kept the Passover were hating the Roman rule and wishing to get rid of it.

Jesus may have been thinking that what they needed more was to get rid of their hatred and bitterness. Certainly he was thinking much about God and asking himself how he could know surely what God wanted for his people.

When the days of the Passover were finished, the people from Nazareth started for home. Again there was the great throng of friends and neighbors journeying along together. Joseph and Mary thought that Jesus was walking with some of the other groups. But when evening came and they stopped to camp for the night, they could not find Jesus anywhere. Then they were frightened. They went straight back to Jerusalem, looking for him. At last they came to the Temple. In one of the Temple courts some of the wisest teachers — teachers who knew most about the sacred books and the law of God — used to sit and let people ask them questions. There, in the midst of them, Mary and Joseph found Jesus. They were glad, and yet a little annoyed. Why had Jesus stayed there and let them be so worried?

"Son," said Mary, "why did you treat us so?"

Jesus was surprised. He thought they should have understood where he would be. "Did you not know," he answered, "that I must be in my Father's house?"

When they were back in Nazareth, Jesus took his place in the home again. But his mother remembered what had happened in Jerusalem, and what Jesus had answered when they asked him why he was in the Temple. The Gospel of Luke tells that she "kept all these things in her heart." The same Gospel says that "Jesus increased in wisdom and in stature, and in favor with God and man." This means that he learned more and more and that he grew taller; that God loved him, and that people loved him too.

After this we do not hear again of Joseph. He may have died about the time Jesus was grown to be a man, or even earlier. But he had given to Jesus more than anyone except Jesus himself could ever know. Always when Jesus thought of God, he did not call him Lord, or the Almighty God. He called him Father. Perhaps the reason for this was that the trust and love between himself and Joseph had shown him what the Father in heaven could be.

After Joseph's death, Jesus took over the carpenter's shop. He was the one now who must support the family. Probably the brothers helped him, as they grew up, and he taught them how to work, as Joseph had taught him. His mother needed him, and so he stayed on in Nazareth year after year. But all the time his thoughts were going a long way beyond Nazareth.

As a boy in the synagogue school, Jesus had read the sacred writings so much that he knew great parts of them by heart. He knew the Ten Commandments, and the rest of the teachings of Moses about how God would have his children live. He had read the writings of the prophets, and he knew how they were always looking forward to the day when God would give his people a savior and a deliverer. He, the Messiah, would be greater than David or any of the kings. And Jesus understood that the greatest of the prophets believed that this Savior would be not for the people of Israel only, but for all the world. He would come not with weapons and with armies to frighten men, but with love, to show them the love of God. And he would make a new world — a world filled with peace and joy.

Often Jesus went out into the quiet of the hills to think and pray. More and more he was understanding now the wonderful message that God was speaking to his mind and heart. He himself must be the Savior. He was the one appointed to show men what God wanted them to be.

Many of the Jews wanted some great soldier who would start a war against the Romans, and free the country from the rule of Rome. But Jesus knew better. He knew that the first thing everyone needed was to be saved from being mean and selfish. As long as everyone thought only of himself, there would be quarreling and bitterness and fighting and war. If men could all think first of the goodness of God, and let God's goodness help them to be brave and kind and generous, then the whole world would be a better place.

CHAPTER THREE

Jesus Begins His Ministry

For many years nothing had been heard of John, Jesus' cousin. Then, all of a sudden, he appeared. His parents must have died long before. John liked to be alone and to think his own thoughts. So he had lived in a part of the country that was a wilderness. Out there in the great wide space the winds seemed to come from the ends of the world; the sun shone down upon the empty land by day; and the stars that no one could count came out like candles in the still sky when it was dark. There John thought of the greatness of God. And the more he thought, the more he was sure that there was something tremendous that he must say.

So one day he left the wilderness where he had lived alone. He went down to the Jordan River, to the place where there were fords in the shallow water, and where many people would be going back and forth. He did not have fine clothes, such as people wore in cities. He was dressed in rough camel skins with a strip of leather about his waist. When people first saw him, with his sunburned face, his fiery eyes, and the quick, bold way in which he moved, they were almost as startled as if they had met a lion. But when he began to speak, they stopped to listen.

"The kingdom of God is at hand," he said. "Repent!"

He meant that they must turn away from their sins, stop doing what was wrong, and put their whole heart into doing what was right.

As news about this strange preacher spread, crowds came from everywhere. They came from as far as Jerusalem, and even from the country beyond it. Men told one another that a new prophet had appeared, a prophet like Elijah. Some even began to wonder whether John might perhaps be more than a prophet. Could he be the one the prophets had said would come at last? Could he be the Messiah?

John said no, he was not the Messiah. He said that his work was to make ready for the Messiah's coming. And he told the people that they should make themselves fit to welcome the Messiah when he did come.

"What shall we do?" asked some men who collected taxes.

"Be honest," said John. "Stop making people pay you more than you know they are supposed to pay."

"What shall we do?" asked some soldiers.

"Stop taking away what belongs to other people," said John. "Live on your wages, and do not try by lies and stealing to get what is not yours."

"And what shall we do?" asked some others.

John told them to be generous. If they had two coats, give one to somebody who did not have any. If they had food to eat, share with the man who had none.

In the crowd around John were some of the priests, and some Pharisees, who were men who knew all about how God ought to be worshiped, but did not always act as though their worshiping had done them any good. The Pharisees were devoted to the law of God as it had come down from Moses and the great teachers and prophets of long ago, and they thought they were faithful to everything the law commanded. But the trouble was that they often forgot the real reasons for the law, and insisted on little points of what they thought was right behavior. They laid down rules telling people exactly how to wash their hands and their dishes, how to dress, and what signs of their religion to wear. They made these things seem almost more important than the Ten Commandments, as though the way a man looked and the little things he did mattered as much as making sure that his life was good and true and kind.

What did John have to say to them? the Pharisees wanted to know. They did not ask this to get an answer. They thought that he would be humble and would say that of course he had no advice to give to such important persons.

John was indignant. These priests were supposed to help people. These Pharisees said their prayers where everyone could see them, but in spite of their pious looks many of them did not love God, or their neighbors either.

"You brood of snakes!" John cried. "Who warned you to try to get away from the punishment that is coming?" He told them there was no use boasting that they were descended from Abraham. If they did not repent and live right, they would be destroyed.

The priests and Pharisees were so angry that they could not

speak. But many of the people were delighted. They had never seen anyone so bold and brave as John. He was not afraid of anything. He must certainly be a prophet sent from God.

John told those who gathered around him that they must be baptized. So they went with him into the river. As the water flowed over them, he prayed that God would make them clean from whatever there was in them that was wrong. He prayed that God would forgive them and help them to make a fresh start toward a better life.

From this time on, John began to be called John the Baptist, and the news of him spread far and wide. It even came to Jesus in the little town of Nazareth. John was preaching about the coming of the kingdom of God that mattered more than anything else to Jesus. So he would go down where John was.

He left Nazareth and went the long way to the fords of the Jordan River. There he saw the crowds gathered around John. He noticed how eagerly they listened. He went nearer to hear what John was saying. And when he saw John baptizing the people, he said that he too wished to be baptized.

John said that Jesus did not need to be baptized by him. But Jesus said, very gently, that John's baptism was for men who loved God and wanted to see his kingdom come. He wanted that too. Then John understood, and he went down into the water with Jesus and baptized him.

When Jesus was baptized, the Holy Spirit of God came to bless Jesus. And into Jesus' heart came a great joy, for the voice of God spoke to him, as a father speaks to his beloved son. At that moment of his baptism, Jesus was made forever certain of what he had begun to know in Nazareth. He knew that God had called him to be the Messiah.

(page 35)

JESUS AND THE FISHERMEN

(page 37) Becher

AT PETER'S HOUSE

Jesus knew that he could not go back again to live in Nazareth.
From this time on, he must give his whole life to telling people
everywhere about God. But first he must be alone to think and
to pray. So he went away into the desert country where for
many years John had been. There was nothing around him but
hills and nothing above him but sky. In the stillness he listened
for the voice of God.

For many days Jesus' mind was so full of his thoughts of God
that he did not think of himself at all. He did not even notice
that he had nothing to eat. Then there seemed to be another
voice speaking. The voice of God had spoken of what was good
and beautiful. This other voice came from someone as real as
if the eyes could see him. Jesus called him the Tempter.

Suddenly Jesus realized how hungry he was.

"Look at all these stones lying on the hillsides," the Tempter
said to Jesus. "Why don't you turn them into bread?"

Yes, if he were God's beloved son, why shouldn't he expect
God to make him able to do something as wonderful as that?

Jesus remembered all the other people who were hungry
much of the time. He had grown up among poor people, and
he knew how many men and women and children there were
who did not always have enough to eat. Suppose that by the
power of God he could provide more food for everybody.
Wouldn't that be the best way for him to begin his work?

That was what the Tempter wanted him to think. But Jesus
knew better. "Men cannot live by bread alone," he answered.

Then the Tempter tried again. He showed Jesus a vision
of the world as it was, and the world as it might be. It was as
though the Tempter had taken Jesus to the top of a mountain
so high that all the kingdoms of the earth were spread out below
him. "All these I will give you," said the Tempter, "if you will
worship me."

But Jesus knew that he could not bring God's kingdom by the Tempter's way. The only way he could change the world was by making men want to be better in their hearts.

"Get behind me, Satan!" he said, "for it is written, Thou shalt worship the Lord thy God, and him only shalt thou serve."

One more temptation was to come; and it was more dangerous because the Tempter pretended that it was no temptation at all.

He seemed to admit that he was beaten. Jesus had chosen right both times. "Since you are God's son," the Tempter said, "and God must love you, then nothing can ever hurt you. God certainly will always keep you safe. Even if you went up to the very highest tip of the great Temple in Jerusalem and threw yourself off into the valley far down below the walls, you could expect the angels of God to come and catch you in their hands."

Jesus understood that the Tempter wanted him to think that he had a right to God's protection — a right that would make everything smooth and safe for him. The Tempter wanted Jesus to think that God would never let him suffer.

But Jesus would not test God's goodness by whether or not God made things safe and easy for him. Perhaps what God had for him to do would be hard and dangerous. That did not matter. The one thing Jesus wanted was that God should make him ready to meet whatever came with glad, unfailing courage.

"You shall not make trial of the Lord your God," Jesus said.

Now all the temptations were ended. Jesus had made the great decisions which he had come into the lonely country to think through. The Tempter slunk away.

Jesus left the wilderness and went back to where people were. And as he went, it seemed that angels were walking at his side.

CHAPTER FOUR

By the Lake of Galilee

After his baptism and the temptations, Jesus went back north to Galilee. He stopped at the city of Capernaum, which was by the shore of the beautiful Lake of Galilee. In Capernaum lived two brothers, Andrew and Peter. One day as Jesus walked along the shore he saw the two men wading in the shallow water. They were fishermen and they were throwing a net for fish

"Come with me," said Jesus, "and I will make you fishers of men."

And they left their nets and followed Jesus.

When he had gone a little farther, Jesus saw two other

brothers. Their names were James and John, and they were the sons of Zebedee. They were fishermen too. They were in a boat with their father, mending their nets. Jesus called to them. Immediately they left their father in the boat with the hired servants to help him, and got out on the shore and came to Jesus. Then all four men, Peter and Andrew and James and John, went with Jesus. Probably they did not think that day that they were leaving their fishing boats for always. All these fishermen knew was that when Jesus asked them to come with him they wanted to go.

These four were Jesus' first disciples. His disciples were men who would love him and stay with him and learn from him and try to do what he wanted them to do.

When Jesus told Andrew and Peter, and James and John that he would make them fishers of men, he meant that they would help him to bring people into the kingdom of God. He was ready now to preach everywhere in Galilee. He began to tell people, "The time has come. The kingdom of God is at hand. Repent, and believe the gospel."

In some ways that was the same message John had preached. But yet it was different. Jesus and John both said that the world could not be a better place until men let God rule their hearts. But John was fierce and stern, and most of the time he told men how bad they were. Jesus did not say much about that. He did not preach so much about men's badness as about God's goodness. He made people feel that God was on their side. Because Jesus trusted them perhaps they could begin to live up to what he seemed to expect. No wonder that what he preached was called the gospel, the "good news."

It was not only what Jesus said that made people excited and glad. It was also what he did. Jesus loved people, and he was sorry for those who were sick or sad. He knew that wonderful things could happen to those who had faith in God. And he knew that he was sent by God to help and to heal.

On the first Sabbath Day after Jesus came to Capernaum, he went into the synagogue. There he healed a man who was out of his mind. All the people were astonished. "What is this?" they asked one another. "Here is a new authority."

The man in the synagogue was not the only person whom Jesus healed that day. When Jesus left the synagogue, he went to Peter's house. Peter's wife's mother was sick in bed with a fever. Jesus went in where she was and took her hand and lifted her up.

"My fever is gone!" she cried, and she came out immediately and helped to get the dinner.

By this time the whole town was talking of Jesus. By the end of the day the sick people from all around were brought to Peter's door. Jesus healed them as he had healed the others.

The next morning, after the long day in Capernaum, Jesus was up early. Before the sun rose he went out into the quiet country beyond the town to pray. When he prayed, he was close to God, and God gave him the steadiness and strength he needed to help people.

When Peter and the others woke, they did not know where Jesus was. They went to look for him. When they found him, they said, "Everyone is searching for you."

And he said to them, "Let us go on to the next towns, that I may preach there also."

So Jesus and his four disciples went on to other towns. Always Jesus preached about the kingdom of God, and of how men must try to make themselves fit to belong to it. Many of those who listened to him had heard the sacred writings read in the synagogue. These people knew at least a little of what Jesus meant. They knew that ever since the time of the prophets men had been hoping that God's kingdom would come, and his will be done on earth. But Jesus made this kingdom seem much more real and near.

Often Jesus had a special way of helping people to understand what he wanted them to learn about God and the kingdom of God. He would point out to them something that they could see, or he would remind them of something they knew already. Then he would tell them that the truth he was teaching was like that. This is what it means when it says in the Gospels that Jesus taught in parables.

One of his parables was the parable of the sower. Perhaps at the very moment when Jesus was speaking, people could look and see with their own eyes what he was talking about. For across a plowed field on a day in the springtime a man was walking, scattering seed. What happened then? Would all the seed grow up into grain? No, said Jesus, they knew very well that it would not. The birds were flocking down and snatching up some of the seed almost before it touched the ground. Some was falling where the earth was full of stones, and where the seed could send down only shallow roots. So when the seed sprang up it would have no strength, and the hot suns would wither it. Some of the seed was falling where weeds also were growing, and presently the weeds would choke it. But where the seed fell on good ground, well plowed and soft and clean, there it would grow up thick and strong. It would ripen into a harvest a hundred times as great as the grain that had been sown.

That is how it may be with people, said Jesus. The words of God are like seeds. If people let them fall into their minds and hearts and stay there, they will grow up into good living. But if their minds are filled with flighty thoughts that flock around like untamed birds, then the thoughts that God sends may be snatched away. Sometimes people are stubborn and the word of God is like the seed that can take no root because it is on stony ground. And sometimes when people think that they do welcome the word of God, and when for a while at least it seems to be springing up in them, then the weeds of little wrong things may grow thick around it, until at length it is covered up and forgotten. But if people really want what God will give them, then they can be like the field made ready, where God's word will strike deep root and grow up into goodness every day.

Jesus also taught the people that the kingdom of God could come to them in little beginnings. Once the spirit of it had entered into their hearts, it would spread and grow like the yeast a woman kneads into flour to make bread. There is just a tiny bit of yeast, compared with the quantity of flour, he told them. But soon that little yeast has spread all through the dough, and every part of it begins to rise.

Again he taught them that when God means anything to happen, people do not need to stand around and watch for it anxiously. God's promises are like the grain sown in the field. It keeps on growing, though no one knows how. It grows in sunlight and in rain, in the daytime and through the night. So, Jesus said, the quiet power of God's spirit can fill men's lives with brightness and with joy.

Somewhere on one of the hillsides above the blue waters of the Lake of Galilee Jesus sat one day. People were gathered around him, and he taught them of God, and of how God would have them live. The words he spoke that day are written in the Gospel of Matthew and are called the Sermon on the Mount.

Jesus began with short sentences which tell the kinds of people who are blessed by God:

"Blessed are the poor in spirit, for theirs is the kingdom of heaven.

"Blessed are those who mourn, for they shall be comforted.

"Blessed are the meek, for they shall inherit the earth.

"Blessed are those who hunger and thirst for righteousness, for they shall be satisfied.

"Blessed are the merciful, for they shall obtain mercy.

"Blessed are the pure in heart, for they shall see God.

"Blessed are the peacemakers, for they shall be called sons of God.

"Blessed are those who are persecuted for righteousness' sake, for theirs is the kingdom of heaven."

The people who listened to Jesus and looked into his face understood what he meant them to remember. The one sure way to be glad is to deserve God's blessing. And the people who will deserve his blessing are those who are not puffed up and conceited, who are gentle and patient, who want to be good more than they want anything else, whose hearts are full of kindness, who carry friendliness wherever they go, and who, when some would try to make them do wrong, keep on steadily and bravely doing right.

Jesus taught the people that the wrong things a person does start with wrong thoughts, and so everyone must watch how he thinks. The law which they had all learned commanded, "Thou shalt not kill," but Jesus said they must try first not to lose their temper.

He told them too that they must be different from the Pharisees. The Pharisees liked to pray standing in the market place, where they thought everyone would see them and admire them for seeming so religious. When they gave money to poor people, they liked to give it where everyone would notice.

Jesus said that neither praying nor doing kindnesses meant anything if they were done for men to see. If there was real kindness, God would know it. When a person really wanted to pray, he should go into a quiet place by himself. There he would be thinking only of God. Jesus taught that prayer was asking God very simply for his blessing and his help. He gave his disciples a prayer which men and women and children all over the world have learned to say:

> "Our Father who art in heaven,
> Hallowed be thy name.
> Thy kingdom come,
> Thy will be done,
> On earth as it is in heaven.
> Give us this day our daily bread;
> And forgive us our debts,
> As we forgive our debtors;
> And lead us not into temptation,
> But deliver us from evil."

And to remind ourselves that what we have prayed in the Lord's Prayer can come true, we say to God at the end:

> "For thine is the kingdom,
> And the power,
> And the glory forever.
>   Amen."

Those who are loving, Jesus said, will know the love of God. They will know, too, that they can trust his goodness.

"Look at the birds of the air," he said. "They neither sow nor reap nor gather into barns, and yet your heavenly Father feeds them."

He told them not to worry about clothes. The lilies in the

fields, he said, grow up from the common ground. Yet God has made them more beautiful than the splendid robes of rich King Solomon. If God feeds the birds, and makes the lilies beautiful, he will surely take care of his children. Good fathers here on earth give their children what they need, and so would their heavenly Father.

It was no wonder that crowds of people came to hear Jesus. He made them feel that God loved them, and that they all could be better than they were.

But there were some people who did not want to hear Jesus. One day he went back to his own town of Nazareth. When the Sabbath came, he went, as he always did, to the service in the synagogue. At the time for the reading from the sacred books, Jesus was asked to choose a chapter and to read it. Jesus turned to the Book of Isaiah and he read to all the people:

"The Spirit of the Lord is upon me, because he has anointed me to preach good news to the poor. He has sent me to proclaim release to the captives, and recovering of sight to the blind, to set at liberty those who are oppressed, to proclaim the acceptable year of the Lord."

When he had finished reading, Jesus told the people that what Isaiah had written was already coming true. In other towns of Galilee people had flocked to hear him. Many who were sad and many who were sick had come to him because he brought them help and strength from God.

But the men and women there in Nazareth, instead of being glad, were angry. Who was Jesus that the people in other places should think he was so important? Hadn't they known him all those years when he lived in their own town? Hadn't he grown up among them? And now why should he be preaching to them? Did he think he was greater than they?

It made Jesus sad to think that he was not wanted by his neighbors of Nazareth and that they would not let him help them

"No prophet is acceptable in his own country," he said. He reminded them that this had been true before. It was outside of Israel that Elijah had healed the son of a widow, a little boy who was about to die. It was not a man from Israel, but Naaman, the Syrian, who had faith enough to come to the prophet Elisha to be cured of leprosy.

When he told them that, the people were angrier than ever. They rose up muttering and crowded him out of the synagogue. Some of them began to shout to one another that they ought to take him up to the edge of a steep rock at the top of the hill and push him over. But Jesus looked them straight in the eyes and they drew back. He walked through the crowd that did not quite dare to touch him, and went his way. So far as we know, he never came back to Nazareth again.

CHAPTER FIVE

People Who Needed Jesus

Near Capernaum, many people were waiting for Jesus. More and more people were coming to him, especially when they were in trouble.

There was a man named Jairus who was a leader in the synagogue. When he caught sight of Jesus, he ran and threw himself at Jesus' feet. He said, "My little daughter is at the point of death. Come and lay your hands on her, so that she may be made well and live."

Jesus started to go with Jairus. A curious crowd followed them. In the crowd was a woman who had been ill for years. She had gone to many doctors and had spent all the money she had. But instead of being made better she had only grown worse. She crowded in to where Jesus was and reached out to try to touch his clothes. "If I can touch even his garments, I shall be made well," she said to herself. And when she did touch him, instantly she felt that something wonderful had happened. Her sickness was gone, and she was well again.

Jesus turned around. "Who was it that touched me?" he asked.

His disciples were surprised that he should ask such a question. "The people are crowding all about," they said. "How can you ask, 'Who touched me?'"

But Jesus said that he knew some special one had touched him. And he looked at the faces of those who were near.

Then the woman, trembling, fell at his feet and told him what had happened.

"Daughter, your faith has made you well," he said to her. "Go in peace, and be healed of your disease."

While they were hurrying toward Jairus' house, messengers came and told Jairus, "Your daughter is dead. There is no use troubling the Master any more."

But Jesus said to Jairus, "Do not fear. Only believe."

He made the crowd stand back and, taking with him only Jairus and Peter and James and John, he went on. When they came close to Jairus' house they saw many people weeping and wailing.

"Why do you act this way?" said Jesus. "The little girl is not dead, but sleeping."

They looked at him with scorn. What did he mean by telling them that she was not dead?

Jesus sent them all away except Jairus and his wife and his three disciples. Then he went into the room where Jairus' daughter lay. He took her by the hand and said to her, "Little girl, I say to you, arise!"

Immediately she stirred, then got up and began to walk. Her father and mother stood there, amazed and overjoyed. Jesus told them to give her something to eat.

So it was that wherever Jesus went he was helping people out of their troubles.

One day he met on the road a man who had leprosy. This was a terrible disease. People were so afraid of lepers that they made them stand off at a distance when anyone approached. And the lepers must give a warning cry, "Unclean! Unclean!"

But this leper ran and knelt down at Jesus' feet. "Lord, if you will, you can make me clean," he said. Jesus healed him. Then Jesus warned him not to tell the crowd. But the man who had been a leper was so excited that he spread the news everywhere. After that, so many people tried to see Jesus that the towns were crowded wherever he went.

One day when Jesus was in Capernaum the news got about that he was there. He began to talk to those who crowded into the house where he was staying. Presently there were so many people that no one else could get in the door.

Now there was a paralyzed man who had some good friends. These friends had made up their minds that they would somehow get the poor man to where Jesus was. So they picked him up as he lay on his mat and brought him to the house. When they saw that there was no chance of carrying him in to Jesus through all that mass of people, they went up the steps to the flat roof of the house. They pried loose some of the tiles that covered the roof. They began to let the man down with ropes through the hole. The people inside looked up astonished as the paralyzed man, lying on his mat, appeared right in front of Jesus.

What Jesus said at first surprised those who were watching.

"Son," he said, "your sins are forgiven." Then he added, "So that you may know that the Son of Man has authority on earth to forgive sins, I say to you, Rise, take up your mat, and go home." And to the amazement of everyone, the paralyzed man got up, rolled up his mat, and left.

When the people first heard Jesus call himself the Son of Man, they may have wondered why he took that name. But the ones who knew the sacred writings could remember that the prophet Ezekiel had heard the voice of God say to him, "Son of Man, stand upon thy feet, and I will speak to thee." And in the Book of Daniel the Son of Man is spoken of as one who would come with the glory of God, to have a kingdom that should never be destroyed.

Some of the scribes who heard Jesus speak of himself as the Son of Man when he healed the paralyzed man were much offended. Scribes spent their lives copying down and learning all the law of Moses, and all that the teachers, or rabbis, had taught about the law since Moses' time. They knew a great deal about the old ways, but they were dull and slow to see that something which had never been known before might come true now. When Jesus said to the paralyzed man, "Your sins are forgiven," the scribes were shocked. Who had ever heard of sins being forgiven by anyone except by God? They could not see that it was the love of God in Jesus which made him able to heal men's sicknesses and to free people from their sins.

From this time on, Jesus knew that the scribes were suspicious of him and always watching him. He felt that some day they would begin to hate him and try to harm him. The strange thing was that these were men who thought that they were good, and who felt certain that they were serving God. It never occurred to them that there might be better and more beautiful ways of serving God than they knew about.

One Sabbath Day some of the scribes and Pharisees had followed Jesus into the synagogue. Among the people in the synagogue there was a man whose hand was crippled. The scribes and Pharisees saw Jesus look at him, and saw his eyes light up with pity. They watched to see what he would do. They knew that the Ten Commandments said that men should not work on the Sabbath Day. The rabbis had taught exactly what was to be called work. They called healing work, and so healing was forbidden on the Sabbath Day.

From the looks on their faces, Jesus could tell what these scribes and Pharisees were thinking. Because they were so hardhearted, his anger blazed like fire. He called to the man who had the shriveled hand, "Come forward!" Then he turned to the scribes and Pharisees. "Is it lawful on the Sabbath Day to do good or to do harm?" he demanded. "To save life or to kill?" The scribes and Pharisees looked at him sullenly, and said nothing.

Then Jesus spoke again to the crippled man. "Stretch out your hand."

He stretched it out, and it was as strong and straight as the other.

But the scribes and Pharisees were not glad. Instead, they were angry, because Jesus had put them to shame. They would not forget this! They went out and began to think and talk of how they might get rid of Jesus. They knew that by themselves they could not manage that, but they thought that perhaps there might be others who would help. They went off and began to talk with some of the men who had influence with the rulers of Galilee. These rulers might be persuaded to stop Jesus' preaching to the people.

Soon afterward they heard of something else which they did not like. Jesus was going by a place where the Roman taxes were collected. The collector was a man named Matthew. Now the

Becher

JESUS TEACHES HIS DISCIPLES

(page 46)

A SICK MAN IS BROUGHT TO JESUS

Pharisees and scribes despised all tax collectors. They thought that no respectable person would have anything to do with a tax collector. But Jesus saw each man for what he really was. He said to Matthew what he had said to Simon Peter and Andrew and James and John, "Follow me."

The people who were standing about must have wondered whether Matthew would go. They supposed that a tax collector liked his business too much to give it up. But Matthew did not hesitate. When he looked at Jesus, he knew that he wanted to follow him, and he did.

Matthew became the fifth of Jesus' disciples. Not long afterward, Jesus chose some other men to be with him, so that altogether there were twelve disciples. The names of the others were Philip and Bartholomew and Thomas and another James and Thaddeus and another Simon and Judas Iscariot.

Matthew had a dinner at his house for Jesus, and invited all his friends.

"How is this?" the scribes and Pharisees asked the disciples. "What does Jesus mean by eating and drinking with tax collectors and sinners?"

When Jesus heard, he gave an answer that has never been forgotten. "Those who are well have no need of a physician, but those who are sick," he said. "I have not come to call the righteous, but sinners to repentance."

In his teaching, Jesus tried to help men see that being good is not following old ideas that never change. God may have new ways for men to live. Jesus said that the scribes and Pharisees who tried to turn the truth upside down, and to say that what he did was evil, were speaking against the goodness of God. If men were being healed in ways which everyone could see were good, then it must be the goodness of God that caused the healing.

About this time trouble came to John the Baptist. John had been preaching boldly. He told the truth, no matter whom it touched. Herod, king in Galilee for the Romans, was a son of the Herod who had been king when Jesus was born. Like his father, he was a man who did what he pleased, even when it was wicked. He had married Herodias, his own brother's wife, and John had said plainly that this was a great sin. Herod arrested John and put him in prison.

There in prison, lonely as he was, John began to wonder what Jesus was doing. Was he really the Messiah for whom John had hoped?

So John sent two of his friends to Jesus to ask, "Are you the Promised One, or must we wait for another?"

At that very time crowds of people, some of them blind and some of them sick, were gathered around Jesus, and he was healing them. Jesus said to the messengers from John, "Go and tell John what you hear and see: the blind receive their sight and the lame walk, lepers are cleansed and the deaf hear, and the dead are raised up, and the poor have good news preached to them."

When the messengers were gone, Jesus turned to the crowd and began to talk to them about John. "When you went out into the wilderness to listen to John," he asked, "what did you expect to see? Someone in fine clothes? No, the people who wear fine clothes are in kings' houses. But what did you really go to see? A prophet? Yes, I tell you, and more than a prophet. For John is the one of whom it was written, 'Behold, I send my messenger before thy face, who shall prepare thy way before thee.' "

Soon after this the wicked Herod had John killed. John's friends buried him. Then they went and told Jesus what had happened.

From that time on, Jesus knew that his life too was in danger. People were going to Herod and telling Herod what Jesus was preaching. They made Herod jealous and uneasy. He wondered if Jesus was beginning to have more power over the people than he had. As he heard more and more of Jesus and of what he did, Herod was afraid.

Some of the Pharisees came to Jesus and told him that he had better go somewhere out of Herod's reach, or Herod would kill him. They did not want to protect Jesus, but they hoped that this might make him stop preaching to the people. But Jesus answered, "Go and tell that fox that I will keep on with my work today and tomorrow and the day following and until my work is done."

The scribes and Pharisees were becoming much disturbed because crowds flocked to Jesus. These teachers of the people said that Jesus was not strict enough about the law of Moses, and that he had no business to heal on the Sabbath Day. They thought it was more important to be correct than to be kind.

The Pharisees and scribes were offended that Jesus did not seem to keep different kinds of people in their proper places. Surely, they thought, no respectable person ought to associate with sinners. Yet there was Jesus, sitting down in Matthew's house with the ragtag and bobtail of the town, and actually saying that what he wanted most to do was to make people like this know that they belonged to God.

Worst of all, Jesus always seemed to be forgetting that the people of Israel were better and more important than any other people. Jesus acted as though he did not remember that they were the children of Abraham and belonged especially to God. Because men and women were human beings and needed him, Jesus treated everyone alike, no matter who they were — even the despised Samaritans.

One of the longest and kindest talks that Jesus had was with a woman of Samaria. In the Gospel of John it is told how once when Jesus was traveling through the Samaritan country, on his way between Jerusalem and Galilee, he stopped to rest at Jacob's well. A woman from the town nearby came out to draw water. When Jesus asked her to let him drink from her water jar, she was astonished. She had never heard of a Jew even speaking to a Samaritan! But when Jesus spoke to her again, and she looked into his face, she lost her shyness. Almost before she knew it, she was telling him all about herself and her troubles.

As Jesus talked, the Samaritan woman began to see what she had never understood before. She had never thought much about God and about how God cared for her, and so she was discouraged and unhappy. Jesus made her know for the first time that God did not have to be worshiped only in the Temple in Jerusalem, or in the Samaritans' own temple, which they said was the right place. He told her that God could be with her in her own heart and in whatever she was doing. When the woman went back to the town, thinking new thoughts, she felt that she was taking with her something more than water from the well.

Jesus was always noticing the particular person who had need of him. The same Gospel of John says that Jesus went several times to Jerusalem to the Passover, or to some other great festival of the Jewish year. Once he came to a place called the Pool of Bethesda. It was believed that at a certain time every day an angel stirred the water of this pool, and whatever sick person stepped into it first after that would be cured. A paralyzed man was there. He had come again and again for years and years. But he had no one to help him, and so when he tried to get into the water, someone else always stepped in before him. Jesus told the man that he should be healed, and healed now, without going into the pool. "Rise up and walk," said Jesus, and the man got up, cured.

Another story in the Gospel of John tells of a man who had been blind ever since he was born. He sat begging on a street of

Jerusalem when Jesus came along. Jesus put clay on the blind man's eyes, and told him to go to the Pool of Siloam and bathe them. The blind man groped his way there. When he washed the clay from his eyes, he could see, for the first time in his life.

Everybody in Jerusalem had known this man and known that he had always been blind. After his healing, some of the chief Pharisees sent for him. They asked him how he had been healed. Who was this Jesus who had healed him? What did he think of Jesus? All the blind man could do was to tell them simply what had happened.

Then the Pharisees called his father and mother, and wanted to know what they had to say. The parents said that all they knew was that the man was their son, that he had been born blind, and that now he could see.

The Pharisees, more and more annoyed, called the man again. "Give God the praise," they said. "The man who healed you is a sinner." They said this because this healing had been done on the Sabbath Day. The man answered that he did not know anything about that. All he knew was that he had been blind, and that now he could see. And he said that anyone who could heal a blind man's eyes must have been given power from God. And he did not understand how such a man could be a sinner.

At that, the Pharisees were indignant. "Are you trying to teach us?" they cried. And they drove him out.

Jesus heard of this, and he found the man. When the man who had been blind saw Jesus, he fell down at his feet and worshiped him. Jesus said, "I came into this world that those who do not see may see." He added that he had also come to show that some of those who thought they saw were really blind.

His words were repeated to the Pharisees. "What does he mean?" they asked. "Is he trying to say that we are blind?" And they were even more angry.

One day Jesus had a message from a Roman centurion, the captain of a company of soldiers that was stationed in Galilee. This man had been friendly to the Jewish people. He had even made a gift toward the building of a synagogue in Capernaum. A servant of his was sick, and he asked some of the leading men of the synagogue to go to Jesus and beg him to come and heal the sick man.

Jesus started toward the centurion's house. But before he reached there, some friends came out to meet him with another message. They told him that the centurion asked him not to trouble himself to come all the way. The centurion felt that he was not good enough to have Jesus come under his roof or even to be in Jesus' presence. He said that he himself was used to giving orders and to having men go or come as he said. He believed that Jesus did not need to come to where the sick man was. If Jesus would only say the word, he knew that his servant would be healed.

Jesus said to the people around him that he had never known a man with as much faith as that, not even among the Jews. And when the messengers went back to the centurion's house, they found that his servant had been healed.

Jesus liked to help not only sick people but well people, too. Once, when he was in the open country away from the towns, crowds kept coming to listen to him. After they had been there for a long time, Jesus said to his disciples that all these people must be growing hungry. Some of them had come a long way and there was no place nearby where they could buy food.

"How much bread have you?" Jesus asked the disciples.

They looked around and did not see anything to eat at all. But Andrew came to Jesus and said, "There is a lad here who has five barley loaves and two fish." That was something, but certainly not much. How could so little feed so many?

"Make the people sit down," said Jesus.

When they were all seated, he took the bread and fish which the little boy put into his hands, and he thanked God. Then he told the disciples to divide the food among the people. The disciples did what Jesus commanded and handed out the food they had. Somehow, as they did this, there was always more, so that all the people were fed, and there was even food left over.

The disciples thought and talked much among themselves of that. It seemed to them that nothing could be too wonderful to expect of Jesus.

That evening he told them all to get into the boat and to go back across the lake to the other side from where they were. But he went up on a hill to pray.

When night came, a wind began to blow against them on the lake, and they were pulling hard on the oars. In the darkness they could not tell where they were. They might be in the middle of the lake. They might be driven where the boat would be smashed on the shore. They did not know.

Suddenly they looked up and were startled. Who was that they saw? Was it Jesus? Then they heard his voice, "Take heart, it is I. Do not be afraid." There he was. He got into the boat with them, and the wind went down.

Another night when the disciples were on the lake and Jesus was with them, there came a sudden storm. The waves began to run so high that they broke across the boat. As water poured in, the disciples were afraid that at any moment they might be sinking. Jesus had lain down in the stern of the boat, and he was sleeping as though nothing at all were happening. In their fright they called him. "Master," they cried, "don't you care if we drown?"

Jesus woke and looked at them, and then he looked out on the lake where the fierce wind lashed the water angrily and the spray was flying. "Peace, be still," he said.

All of a sudden the wind dropped and the waves flattened and the boat came to the shore. "Why were you afraid?" he said. "Do you have no faith?"

The disciples were filled with awe and wonder, and after that they felt that they would be safe anywhere if only Jesus were there too.

By now the disciples had been with Jesus long enough to begin to do some of the work among people which he had shown them that God wanted done. So Jesus sent them out, two by two, to preach in the neighboring towns. Here and there among the cities and villages of Galilee they went, and presently they came back to Jesus full of joy. They told him that he had made them have a power that was greater than the evil spirits of sickness and sin. They had been able to help people and to heal them as they had seen him do.

CHAPTER SIX

What Jesus Taught and Did

"The common people heard him gladly," it is said of Jesus in the Gospels. But all the while his enemies were growing more bitter against him. They tried to oppose him in every way they could. Jesus saw that in the end they would have their way. He could not finish what he was doing and live an easy life. More and more he would have to go into danger. He knew that he must be ready even to die, rather than stop his preaching of the love of God.

One day when the disciples were around him Jesus asked them, "Who do the people say I am?"

The disciples gave him different answers. They told him that some people said he was John the Baptist come to life again. Some said he was Elijah. Others said that he must be one of the prophets, they did not know which one.

"But who do you say I am?" Jesus asked.

Then Peter burst out with what he had been thinking, but had never said before. "You are the Christ!" he cried. When he said to Jesus, "You are the Christ," Peter was using the name that meant the same as the Messiah, the one whom God himself had sent to be the Savior of his people.

Jesus told them not to say this yet to anyone else. He knew that the people expected the Messiah to come with great power, like a leader at the head of an army. But their ideas were different from what he knew must be true.

"The Son of Man must suffer much," he told his disciples. And he went on to say that the time would come when all the leaders of the people and the scribes and chief priests would turn against him, and he would be killed.

Peter was shocked at such a thought. He began to contradict Jesus, and to argue that such a thing could not possibly happen to him. But Jesus looked straight at the disciples. He wanted them to understand that he meant exactly what he was saying. He told Peter that men would expect a person to keep himself from danger, but that this was not the way of God.

He said to his disciples that if they wanted to stay with him, each of them would have to be ready to go into danger. Whoever thought of saving his own life ahead of everything else would lose it, but whoever was willing to lose his life for Christ's sake would save it. The great thing, he told his disciples, was to be brave and true.

Later, he told them that soon he would be going up to Jerusalem, where his enemies would try to put him to death. He would not look out for himself. His work was to do the work of God, no matter what might happen.

But the disciples had not yet learned to be like Jesus. When they were all together in Capernaum, Jesus asked them, "What was it that you were arguing about on the way?" They were ashamed to tell him, for they had been arguing about which of them was the greatest.

Jesus sat down to talk to them. "If any man would like to be first," he said, "he must put himself last, and be the servant of all." Then he took a little child in his arms. He told the disciples that whoever wanted to belong to the kingdom of God must be like a child, not like someone trying to be a great man.

Always Jesus was teaching his disciples that if they were to follow him and grow to be like him, they must think less and less of themselves and more of how they could be just and generous to others.

Once Peter, remembering someone who had done him harm and might do him harm again, asked Jesus how often he would have to forgive this man. "Must I forgive him seven times?" he wanted to know.

Jesus answered, "I do not say seven times, but seventy times seven." He meant that Peter must not set any limits at all to his forgiveness. He must always be ready to forgive.

Jesus told the disciples that whenever they were kind they could know most surely that they were beginning to be what he would have them be. If they even gave a cup of cold water to someone who was thirsty, they would find a blessing.

To make people know the love of God for even the least important person, Jesus told three parables.

He said: "Which one of you, if he has a hundred sheep and has lost one of them, does not leave the ninety-nine out in the open, and go after the lost sheep until he finds it? When he does find it, he takes it up on his shoulder, rejoicing. And when he comes home, he calls together his friends and neighbors and says to them, 'Rejoice with me, for I have found my sheep that was lost.'

"So, I tell you, there shall be more joy in heaven over one sinner who repents than over ninety-nine righteous people who did not need to repent."

Again Jesus said: "Or what woman who has ten silver coins and loses one, does not light a lamp and sweep the house, and look everywhere until she finds it. And when she does find it, she calls her friends and neighbors and says, 'Rejoice with me, for I have found the coin I lost.'

"In the same way there is joy among the angels of God over one sinner who repents."

Then Jesus told one of the most beautiful parables of all— the story of the son who thought that the way to be happy was to leave his father's home and go wherever he liked.

Jesus said: 'There was a man who had two sons. The younger one said to his father, 'Father, give me now what will belong to me later on.'

"So his father gave it to him

"Not many days later, the younger son gathered up all he owned, and went on a journey to a country a long way off. There he wasted his money foolishly. When he had spent everything, he began to be in want. So he went to work for a man of that country who sent him into his fields to feed the pigs. Then this young son who had left his father's home was so hungry that he would have been glad to fill his stomach with the pods the pigs ate. At last one day he came to his senses. He said, 'How many servants of my father have bread enough and to spare, and I perish here with hunger! I will arise and go to my father, and I will say to him, "Father, I have sinned against heaven and before you; I am no more worthy to be called your son; treat me as one of your hired servants." '

"So he arose and came to his father. But while he was yet a great way off, his father saw him and ran and took him in his arms and kissed him. The son said to him, 'Father, I have sinned against heaven and before you; I am no longer worthy to be called your son.'

"But his father said to the servants, 'Bring quickly the best robe, and put it on him. Put a ring on his hand, and shoes on his feet. Bring the fatted calf and kill it, and let us eat and make merry. For this my son was dead, and is alive again; he was lost, and is found!' And they began to be merry.

"Now the elder son was in the field. As he came near the house, he heard music and dancing. He called one of the servants and asked what all this meant.

"The servant said to him, 'Your brother has come, and your father has killed the fatted calf, because he is back home safe and sound.'

"This made the elder son angry, and he would not go in. Then his father came out and entreated him. But he answered his father, 'Look. These many years I have served you, and I never disobeyed your command; yet you never gave me a kid, that I might make merry with my friends. But when this son of yours came, who has wasted your money, you have killed for him the fatted calf!'

" 'Son,' his father said, 'you are always with me, and all that is mine is yours. It was right to make merry and be glad, for this your brother was dead, and is alive again; he was lost, and is found.' "

Jesus not only taught about the love of God, even for those who had done wrong, but he showed in the way he lived what that love of God could mean.

Once he was invited to dinner at the house of a man named Simon, who was a Pharisee. Simon was one of the few Pharisees who would have anything to do with Jesus. Perhaps he asked Jesus to his house out of curiosity, for at first he did not treat his guest with much politeness. People's feet became very dusty after they had walked along the roads, because they wore open sandals. So it was the custom when a guest came in — especially a guest whom the master of the house wished to honor — to have a servant bring a basin of water and wash his feet. But Simon did not trouble to arrange for that.

During the dinner a woman from the streets came into Simon's house. She went to where Jesus was sitting and knelt beside him, weeping. As her tears fell upon his feet, she wiped the tears away with her long hair. Then she poured on his feet precious perfume that she had brought in an alabaster jar.

When Simon saw that Jesus let her do that, he said to himself, "If this man were a prophet, he would know that this woman is a sinner."

Jesus knew what Simon was thinking. "Simon," he said, "I have something to say to you."

"What is it?" asked Simon.

Jesus said: "There were once two men who owed another man money. One of them owed him ten times as much as the other. When they could not pay, the man forgave the debts of both of them. Which of those two men do you think would love him more?"

Simon said that he supposed it would be the one who had owed more and to whom more had been forgiven.

Jesus told him that was the right answer. Then he said, "I

entered your house, and you gave me no water for my feet. But this woman has wet my feet with her tears and wiped them with her hair. You gave me no kiss, but from the time I came in she has not ceased to kiss my feet, and she has put perfume on them also. Therefore, I tell you, her sins, which are many, are forgiven, for she loved much; but he who loves little is forgiven little."

Those who were at the table with him began to whisper among themselves, "Who is this who thinks he can forgive sins?"

But Jesus said to the woman, "Your faith has saved you; go in peace."

CHAPTER SEVEN

On the Way to Jerusalem

The time had come for Jesus to leave Galilee. He must leave most of his friends and the people who loved him. He must leave the beautiful hills and fields he knew so well, and the quiet paths where he used to walk. But the capital of Palestine was the great city of Jerusalem, and it was in Jerusalem that the leaders of the people lived. And so to Jerusalem Jesus must go. He must go to let all who were there understand the message he had come to bring from God.

He took the road that led south through Samaria. Most of the Jews would not go into Samaria if they could help it. They hated

Becher

JESUS HEALS THE SICK

Coleman

JESUS, THE FRIEND OF CHILDREN

the Samaritans, and the Samaritans hated them. But Jesus' heart
was too big to feel that way. He wanted to be a friend to everyone.
The Samaritans did not know that. When they saw him and his
disciples, they thought only of the old grudge they had against
the Jews.

It was the end of the day, and Jesus saw ahead of them a village. He sent two of his disciples to ask if they might all stay there
for the night. But the Samaritans answered rudely. No, Jesus and
his friends could not stay there. When the message was brought
back to Jesus, James and John were so angry that they asked
Jesus why he did not call down fire from heaven to burn up such
a place as that. Jesus rebuked them. He said they ought to know
that he had not come to destroy men's lives, but to save them.
Instead of being angry with the Samaritans, he was sorry for
them. If he had been received into their village, he might have
healed the sick people there and encouraged the unhappy ones.
Men and women and little children might have remembered all
their lives that they had seen him. But now, because of their
ugly feelings, all this was not to be. Jesus went on to another
village, and the village that would not welcome him never knew
what it had lost.

Every now and then, as Jesus and his disciples went on their
way toward Jerusalem, someone would come to Jesus and say
that he wished to become a disciple. Jesus knew that there was no
use for anyone to come with him in a halfhearted way. If a person
wished to come with Jesus, that person must be ready to face
whatever happened. He must want to stand by Jesus more than
he wanted anything else in the world. And he might have to leave
everything else behind.

One day there came to Jesus a young man who was very rich.
He was so anxious to see Jesus that he ran after him until he over-
took him. This young man had a problem on his mind. He wanted

to know how he ought to live. He seemed so eager that when Jesus looked at him, Jesus loved him. He asked the young man if he knew the Ten Commandments. Yes, the young man had known them ever since he was a child, and he had tried to keep them. But Jesus, looking into his eyes, saw that he was restless and unhappy. Jesus understood why. The young man was too fond of his money. It was like a chain, which held him back from doing brave, unselfish things.

"Go, sell all you have," said Jesus, "and give the money to the poor. Then come and follow me."

For a moment the young man almost thought he would do this. Then he hesitated and looked down sadly. He turned and went away. Jesus said to the disciples that it was hard for a rich man to get into the kingdom of God — as hard as it would be for a great, clumsy camel, with a load strapped on his back, to get down on his knees and crawl through a very small gate.

"But that is impossible," they said. "Is it impossible then for any rich man to come into God's kingdom?"

Jesus said that it was impossible as long as a person kept on thinking that his money mattered more than anything else. But if he truly wished it, God could help him let go of the things that held him back.

Another man came to Jesus and said that he wanted to go with him, no matter where that should be. Jesus said to him, "Foxes have holes, and birds of the air have nests; but the Son of Man has nowhere to lay his head."

There were others who said they wanted to follow Jesus. Jesus remembered men he had seen start to work in the fields, and after a while get tired and stop. "No one," he said, "who puts his hand to the plow and looks back is fit for the kingdom of God." He said that no one should start something unless he was determined to see it through. Else he would be like a man who began to build a tower and then, when he found how much it would cost, stopped building, and left it with nothing but the foundations. People coming by would laugh and say, "This man began to build, and was not able to finish."

Another story Jesus told was of a man whose fields brought forth rich crops. There was so much that there was not room in his barns to store all his grain.

"What shall I do?" the man asked himself. He did not think of sharing his grain. Instead, he said, "I know what I will do. I will pull down my old barns and build bigger ones. Then all my grain will be safe. And I can say to myself, 'See, you have enough now for many years. You can take your ease, eat, drink, and be merry.' "

But in God's sight this man was no better than a fool. That very night he died. Then what good to him was all the grain he had gathered?

But still it was hard for even the disciples not to be thinking of what they hoped to gain. If they were not to have riches, then perhaps they would have power and fame.

One day James and John came to Jesus after first looking around to be sure that none of the others were near enough to hear. They said, "Master, we have something we want to ask of you, and we want you to say that you will do it."

Jesus asked them what it was they wanted.

They answered, "Promise us that we may sit beside you, one on your right hand and the other on your left, when you have your kingdom."

Jesus told them that they did not understand what they were asking. Whoever kept close to him would not sit on splendid thrones. They might not have any great honors at all. And they would not have riches or safety. Yet the reward which they would gain at last would be a greater one than they had dreamed of.

But they would have to give themselves devotedly to God's work, no matter what it might cost. Could they do that?

James and John were getting a very different answer from what they had wanted. They had been selfish. But they were brave, too, and they loved Jesus. Yes, they said, they would keep on following him, even though they had no reward, but only risk and danger.

When the other disciples heard what James and John had asked, they were indignant. So James and John had been trying to get ahead of them!

Then Jesus called all the disciples together. He told them that most people who wanted to be great thought they must rule over others. "But it shall not be so among you," he said. "Whoever would be great among you must be your servant, and whoever would be first among you must be servant of all."

On the way to Jerusalem, Jesus and his disciples came to Jericho, on the Jordan River. Outside the city a blind man named Bartimaeus was sitting by the roadside, begging. Bartimaeus could not see, but he could hear the voices of a crowd of people coming toward him and the sound of many feet upon the road.

"What is it? What is happening?" he asked.

"Jesus of Nazareth is passing by," men told him.

Bartimaeus had heard about Jesus. He began to cry out, "Jesus, Son of David, have mercy on me!"

The people nearby did not like all that noise of his. "Stop it!" they said. Why should Jesus be bothered with this blind man?

But Bartimaeus cried all the louder, "Jesus, Son of David, have mercy on me!"

Jesus heard. He said to bring the man to him.

When someone led Bartimaeus to Jesus, Jesus asked, "What do you want me to do for you?"

"Lord," the blind man answered, "let me receive my sight!"

Jesus said to him, "Receive your sight. Your faith has made you well." And immediately Bartimaeus began to see again, and he followed Jesus, shouting with wonder and excitement, and praising God.

Jesus went on into Jericho. In that city lived a man named Zacchaeus. He was very rich, and the reason he was rich was that he was a tax collector. He wanted to see Jesus, but he was very short and could not see over the heads of the crowd. Nobody would make room for him. So he ran ahead and climbed up into a tree. There he could look down and see Jesus as he passed that way.

When Jesus came to the place, he looked up and saw Zacchaeus. "Zacchaeus," he called, "come down." And then he said something which astonished both Zacchaeus and all the people. Jesus told Zacchaeus that he intended to stay at his house that day.

Joyfully Zacchaeus hurried down from the tree. He went ahead to his house and welcomed Jesus there. But the crowd grumbled. Did Jesus know the sort of man Zacchaeus was? Why was he going into the house of a tax collector — a man whom they despised?

The people were judging Zacchaeus by the business he was in. Tax collectors were hateful to the Jews because they took money from them to turn over to the Romans — and often they took more than they should. Most people thought that all tax collectors were bad. But Zacchaeus was better than they knew. And when he saw Jesus, he wanted to be better than he was.

When they were together in Zacchaeus' house, the little tax

collector said to Jesus, "Lord, half of my goods I give to the poor; and if I have ever made any man pay more taxes than he owed, I give it back to him four times over."

Jesus was glad. He understood Zacchaeus although the crowd did not.

"The Son of Man," he told Zacchaeus, "came to seek and to save that which was lost." And he told him that this day God's love was shown to him.

One day a lawyer came to Jesus. This man thought he knew a great deal and was very satisfied with himself. "Master," he said, "tell us what is the greatest commandment of the law?"

Jesus answered, "You shall love the Lord your God with all your heart, and with all your soul, and with all your strength, and with all your mind; and your neighbor as yourself."

"Well, yes," the lawyer answered, "but who is my neighbor?"

He wanted Jesus to say that his neighbors were his family, and his friends, and perhaps the people who lived in the next house, or in the same street. He was willing to be kind to them, but he did not want to bother about other people.

Jesus told the lawyer a story.

He said that once there was a man going along on the road from Jerusalem to Jericho. As he went, robbers sprang out on him. They took all his money and his clothes, and beat him, and left him lying there, half dead.

Then along the road there came a priest. When he saw the wounded man, he stepped over to the other side of the road and went by as though he had not seen the hurt man at all.

A little later there came along a Levite, who was one of the servants of the Temple. He did not stop either. Like the priest he hurried by on the other side.

Then there came a Samaritan. No one would expect a Samaritan to stop and help a Jew. But when this Samaritan saw the wounded man, his heart was full of pity for him. He got down from the donkey he was riding and went straight to the man who was hurt. He put some healing oil on his wounds and bound them up. Then he lifted the man onto his donkey and took him to an inn. The next morning the Samaritan gave some money to the keeper of the inn.

"Take care of this man," the Samaritan said, "and when I come back this way, I will pay you whatever more you may have spent."

"Now," said Jesus, "which one of these three do you think was a neighbor to the man who fell among the thieves?"

The lawyer who had asked Jesus the question about the greatest commandment answered, "I suppose it was the one who showed mercy."

And Jesus said to him, "Go and do as he did."

Jesus told another parable as he looked at people, especially some of the Pharisees, who thought they were very important.

It was the custom at large dinners for men to be seated in the order of their rank. Important people were placed at the head of the table, and unimportant people at the foot. When some of the Pharisees went to a dinner, they walked in expecting to be at the head. That was not the way to do, said Jesus.

"If you are invited to a dinner," he told those who were listening to him, "do not walk up to the top places. If you do that, the host might come and tell you that you do not belong there. Then with shame you would go down to the foot of the table. Instead, when you go in, take the lowest seat. Then the host may come and say, 'Friend, come up higher.'"

Jesus wanted them to understand that in God's sight the

people who push themselves forward are not the ones who have honor.

He wanted them to know, too, that God's love goes out to all people. So Jesus told of a nobleman who made a great feast for his son's wedding and invited all his friends. But they were busy with different things, and they sent back excuses why they could not come. Then the nobleman told the servants to go out into the streets and highways and bring in all the poor and humble folk they could find. The servants did this. And so it was the humble people who sat down to the feast. So it might be, said Jesus, in the kingdom of God.

On the way to Jerusalem, Jesus came to the little town of Bethany. Two sisters, named Martha and Mary, lived there. They were special friends of Jesus, and he was to stay at their house. Martha decided to give him the best supper she could prepare. She worked so hard that soon she was hot and upset. Mary had gone to sit down at Jesus' feet and listen to him. Martha saw her there and was annoyed. Presently she lost her patience altogether, and she said to Jesus, "Tell Mary to come here and help me."

But Jesus knew that Martha had the wrong idea. She thought that getting a big meal was the best thing she could do for Jesus. But Jesus was not so much interested in what he had to eat as in talking over important things with someone eager to understand them. He answered, "Martha, Martha, you are anxious and troubled about many things; but Mary has made a good choice; she has chosen something more important, which shall not be taken away from her."

CHAPTER EIGHT

Jesus Among His Enemies

Now the time had come for Jesus to enter Jerusalem. He decided to go into the city in a way that would make all the leaders of the nation decide whether or not they would receive him as the Messiah sent from God.

Jesus knew that many of the leaders had set themselves against him. In the first place, he was from Nazareth, and they thought that anyone who did not live in Jerusalem could not amount to much. Then they were offended because they had heard that Jesus was not strict about the law, and had done such things as healing on the Sabbath. He went into the homes of the wrong people, and he had even spoken of Samaritans as though they were as good as Jews. Worse still, these leaders were afraid that if more and more people kept on following Jesus, they themselves would get into trouble with the Roman rulers.

For all these reasons they were watching Jesus. As priests and scribes and Pharisees, they were the ones who were supposed to teach the people to be religious. They did tell the people what they ought to do, such as coming to the Temple at the proper times and bringing their offerings and keeping the law. But the more important commandments of God they did not even obey themselves. They were not sorry for people in trouble; they did not try to help poor people; they were not patient with ignorant people; and when someone did wrong, they judged him cruelly. And all the while they pretended to be good. They knew that Jesus was always fearless about speaking the truth. They were afraid that he would expose them to the people. And they had reason to be afraid; for as he looked at them he saw their pious expressions, and yet knew that there was evil in their hearts.

It was on the first day of the week, the Sunday which is remembered as Palm Sunday, that Jesus went into Jerusalem. He wanted everyone there to understand that he was the one sent from God, whose coming was more important than that of anyone who had ever come before. But he did not want anyone to get the wrong idea of the sort of leader he was. Many of the people wanted a leader who would start a war. Jesus was there not to teach men to kill, but to show them how to live. So he would not come in on horseback, as though he were a conqueror at the head of armies.

Jesus remembered that it had been written in the Book of the Prophet Zechariah, "Behold, thy king cometh unto thee . . . lowly, and riding upon an ass." So he sent two of his disciples into a nearby village to untie an ass's colt and bring it to him. He seated himself upon the colt and, with his disciples beside him, he rode along the way that led over the hill of Olivet. At the top of the hill, he looked down on Jerusalem, with its gleaming walls and the towers of the Temple rising against the sky.

Through the streets of the city ran the rumor of what was happening. "Jesus of Nazareth is coming!" men said to one another. A crowd began to hurry out of the city toward the road from Olivet. When they met Jesus, they tore green branches from the trees and spread them on his way.

And they ran beside him and began to chant: "Hosanna! Blessed is he who comes in the name of the Lord. . . . Hosanna in the highest!"

The priests and Pharisees were not in that welcoming crowd. Sullenly they waited in Jerusalem to see what would happen next. But Jesus had not come to take Jerusalem by force. He had come for something much more difficult — to try to change the hearts of men.

He rode to the Temple and entered its courts. When he had looked about, he left and returned to Bethany, full of his own thoughts.

That evening he took his disciples to a height where they could look down again upon Jerusalem. It was so beautiful that it seemed as though it ought indeed to be the Holy City. But Jesus wept as he looked at it. He knew how much wrong and ugliness there was among the important men there. He had come to save them, but they might not let themselves be saved.

"O Jerusalem, Jerusalem!" he cried, "killing the prophets and stoning those who are sent to you! How often would I have gathered your children together as a hen gathers her brood under her wings, and you would not!"

The next day Jesus went again from Bethany into Jerusalem, and up to the Temple courts.

The priests had the right to sell in the Temple the pigeons and the lambs the people bought to use as offerings to God. The priests also had the right to make the people exchange their money for the sacred money which was the only kind they were allowed to use in the Temple courts. By charging high prices, the priests grew rich on this trading, and they were more interested in growing rich than in leading the people in the worship of God.

Jesus was indignant when he saw all this trading going on in the Temple courts. He took some small cords and wove them into a whip. "It is written, 'My house shall be a house of prayer'; but you have made it a den of robbers!" he said to the priests and to the people they had hired to help with the selling. Then he began to drive out the animals and to upset the tables of the moneychangers. When the traders looked at him and saw the expression on his face, they were frightened, and they tumbled over one another in their hurry to get out.

The priests were furious that Jesus was breaking up their business. From that day on, they had such a grudge against him that there was nothing they would not do to get rid of him. Still they did not dare to touch him, for they were afraid of the crowds. Many of the people, knowing Jesus' goodness and admiring his courage, flocked around him.

Every day Jesus went to the Temple courts and taught all who gathered around to listen. But the religious leaders, who ought to have been the first to welcome one who came as the messenger of God, hated Jesus, and they set themselves against him.

"There was once a man who had two sons," Jesus told the people. "He came to one of them and said, 'Son, go and work in my vineyard today'; but the son answered, 'I will not.' But afterward, he changed his mind and went. Then the father came to the other son, and said the same thing to him. This son answered, 'I go, sir.' But he did not go. Which of these two, do you think, obeyed his father?"

Some of the listeners knew that they were like the son who said, "I go, sir," and did not go. Often they had said aloud that they would follow the commandments of God, but they had not followed them. They knew in their hearts that even people who at first had been careless and disobedient, but afterward had been sorry and had tried to do right, were better than they. Still they did not like it when Jesus went on to say, "I tell you, the tax collectors will go into the kingdom of God before you. John the Baptist came to you preaching righteousness, and you did not believe him; . . . neither did you repent and believe him afterward."

He told them another parable: "There was a rich man who planted a vineyard and set a hedge around it, and dug a winepress in it, and built a tower, and let it out to tenants and went into another country. When the harvesttime had come, he sent his servants to the tenants to get what was owed to him. The tenants took his servants and beat one, killed another, and stoned another. Again he sent other servants, and the tenants did the same to them. Afterward the owner of the vineyard sent his son to them, for he said, 'They will respect my son.' But when the tenants saw his son, they said to themselves, 'This is the heir; come, let us kill him and take what would be his.' So they took him and flung him out of the vineyard, and killed him. When the owner of the vineyard comes," said Jesus, "what will he do to those wicked men?"

The listeners saw the answer quickly enough. They said, "He will put those miserable wretches to death, and let out the vineyard to other tenants who will pay him what should belong to him from the harvest."

Jesus rebuked those who were proud and stubborn, but he was quick to praise wherever there was goodness. He saw a woman go up shyly to the offering box in the Temple. She took out two tiny coins, which were all that she had, and she dropped them in. In God's sight, said Jesus, that was a greater offering than the big gifts which had been made by men who had much money. "This poor widow," he said, "has put in more than all of them, for they gave out of their abundance, but she has put in everything that she had."

And he told this story:

"Two men went up into the Temple to pray, one a Pharisee and the other a tax collector. The Pharisee stood and prayed, 'God, I thank thee that I am not like other men. I have not stolen, nor cheated anybody, nor done disgraceful things. I am not like that tax collector. I fast twice every week, and I give to the Temple a tenth of what I own.' But the tax collector, standing at a distance from the holy place, did not think he was good enough even to lift up his eyes to God. He beat upon his breast and cried, 'God, be merciful to me, a sinner.'

"I tell you," said Jesus, "this man went back to his house accepted in God's sight rather than the other; for whoever makes himself great shall be humbled, and whoever humbles himself shall be exalted."

Every day Jesus went up to the Temple and taught. Still the important men would not listen to him. They only tried to trap him with twisted questions. But Jesus could not be trapped. And whether these men listened or not, he told parables which were remembered, and which have been written in the Gospels for us to read.

Jesus said that there was once a rich nobleman who was going away for a long time. He called some of his trusted servants and he gave to one of them five talents. One talent was a great sum of money, but he trusted this servant with five; and he told him to see how well he could use these until his master came back. To the second servant he gave two talents, and to the third servant, one. He told them to use that money as wisely as they knew how.

Two of the men went to work to try to make the money that had been given them earn more. But the third man either did not care or else he thought he would not do anything that would make him run a risk. So he took the one talent, wrapped it up, and hid it.

After a long time the nobleman came back. He called his servants and asked them to give him a report.

The first man said he had taken his five talents and made another five talents. The man who had had two talents said he had earned two talents more. Their master praised both of these men.

Then came the third man, trying to make excuse. He said he was afraid of what might happen if he lost his talent, and so he had wrapped it up carefully and laid it by. And now here it was — everything that he had been given.

But the nobleman was very stern. This man had wasted his chance, and he should not have another. His master took the talent and sent the man away. Then he gave the talent to the man who had done the most with his.

Those who listened understood what Jesus was teaching them. It was that God also will hold men responsible to use well the gifts he has given them.

Jesus told another parable as a warning to people who were careless.

There were ten young girls, he said, who were to be bridesmaids at a wedding. There was a procession in the evening, and they all went out to walk in it, carrying lanterns.

Suddenly five of them found that their lanterns were going out. They had forgotten to bring any oil. They said to the other five girls, "Our lanterns are going out. Give us some of your oil." But the others said they could not, for if they did, they would not have enough for themselves. The five who had been careless would have to go and buy some.

While they were gone, trying to buy the oil, the wedding procession ended and the wedding itself began. When the careless five got back, the door of the house was shut, and the man at the door said that he did not know them, and that they could not come in.

Although priests and scribes and Pharisees hated Jesus, many of the people admired him very much. They thought that it would be an honor to do anything they could for him, and they would be glad to do it. But Jesus told a parable that was full of surprise.

He said the time would come when he would know whether people really had cared for him or not. He would say to them all: "Once I was hungry, and you gave me food. I was thirsty, and you gave me water. I was a stranger, and you invited me in. I was naked, and you gave me clothes. I was sick, and you came to visit me. I was in prison, and you came to help me there." Then they would all be astonished, and they would say: "No, Lord, we never did all those things for you."

But he would answer, yes, that they had really done so. For if they had helped any person at all who was in need, it was just as though they had helped him. Then they were doing exactly

Becher

JESUS TEACHES THE PEOPLE

(page 60) Lee

THE LAMB THAT WAS LOST

what he wanted them to do. They were showing, in the one way that mattered, that they loved him.

It was the week before the holiest time of the year, the festival of the Passover. All the Jews who could possibly do so came up to Jerusalem to celebrate this festival. Every family kept the feast together. The twelve disciples were like Jesus' family now. Jesus told two of them to go ahead of the rest and find a quiet room where they could sit down to supper together. The two disciples found an upper room. Jesus joined them, with the rest of the twelve.

When they were all gathered, the disciples looked at one another. There was no servant to wash their feet, and each man thought to himself that it was not his business to wash the others' feet. Let someone else begin to do it.

Jesus saw what they were thinking. He went and found a basin of water and a pitcher and a towel. Then he began to wash the disciples' feet. They were ashamed, and they did not know what to say. But when he came to Peter, Peter exclaimed, "You shall never wash my feet." Jesus told Peter that it was more than their feet that needed to be washed. Their hearts also needed to be washed from whatever was wrong and selfish.

When he had finished, and they were around the table, Jesus began to talk to them about the love of God, and of the way they ought to live because of it. What Jesus said was told afterward, and some of it was written down in the Gospel of John, beginning with the words, "Let not your heart be troubled; you believe in God, believe also in me."

One thing Jesus said to them was, "A new commandment I give to you, that you love one another, even as I have loved you. . . . By this all men will know that you are my disciples, if you have love for one another."

They ate the Passover supper, just as it had been eaten for

hundreds of years. They had bread without yeast in it, a cup of wine, roasted lamb and bitter herbs, such as the people of Israel had eaten in haste that night, so long before, when Moses led them out of Egypt.

Jesus, knowing that his enemies were plotting against his life, told the disciples that this was the last time he should ever sit down to supper with them on this earth.

This made them sad and silent. But they were shocked into speech when Jesus said, "One of you who is eating with me will betray me." Then one by one they began to ask him, "Is it I, Lord?" Peter cried out that no matter who else might turn against Jesus, he never would. But Jesus told him that on that very night, before the cocks should begin to crow for dawn the next morning, Peter would deny three times that he even knew his Master.

Jesus took the cup of wine and said over it the words of blessing, and passed it to them all. He said that the bread and wine should always be in memory of him as his disciples had known him in this life, and a promise that they should know him in the life to come.

Then he took a piece of bread. He said, "The one to whom I give this bread, when I have dipped it, is the one who will betray me." And as they all sat and held their breath, he dipped the bread in the dish and handed it to Judas.

The other disciples did not know it, but Judas, called Iscariot, had gone to the council of priests and said to them that he would tell them how they could arrest Jesus. He promised to show them where they could find Jesus quickly, before the crowds could learn what they were doing. For this, the priests had paid Judas thirty pieces of silver money.

No one can tell why Judas acted so. Perhaps he was greedy and wanted money, but the money the priests gave him was not much. Or perhaps he had been growing surly and disappointed. He may have thought, as so many of the people did, that Jesus would make himself a king, and then that he, Judas, would be a great person. Little by little he had begun to see that this would not happen.

When Jesus gave the bread to Judas, he got up immediately and went out.

Jesus and the others stayed and talked for a long time. They sang a hymn together and then they left the upper room. They went down to the street and out one of the city gates, to a place called the Garden of Gethsemane. There, under the shadow of olive trees, Jesus told the disciples to sit down and wait for him. He went farther into the garden and kneeled down to pray. He knew now that his enemies were searching for him, and that this time they would stop at nothing. He was looking into the face of death.

"Father," he prayed, "all things are possible to thee." And he asked that he might be delivered from the death that seemed to be drawing near. But then he said, "Yet, not my will, but thine be done."

He came back to where he had left the disciples, and found them lying on the ground asleep.

"Peter," he said, "are you asleep? Could you not watch one hour?" Then pityingly he added, "Your spirit is willing, but your flesh is weak."

Again Jesus went off and prayed. When he returned, the disciples were asleep again.

A third time it was the same way. "Are you still sleeping and taking your rest?" he asked. "The hour has come. The Son of Man is betrayed into the hands of sinners. Rise, let us be going; see, my betrayer is at hand."

At that moment there was a noise of voices and of feet. Through the darkness came men with swords and clubs. At their head was

Judas. He had told them that he would give them a sign by which they could know which one was Jesus.

Judas went straight to Jesus and kissed him. "Master!" he said.

Jesus looked at him. "Judas," he asked, "would you betray the Son of Man with a kiss?"

Then the men who had been sent to arrest Jesus took him and led him away. They led him to the hall where the great council of the priests and rulers, which was called the Sanhedrin, was meeting.

But all the disciples scattered and fled. Only Peter followed at a distance. He crept into the court outside the hall of the Sanhedrin. Presently he came close to a fire and sat there, warming himself. One of the maidservants caught sight of his face. "You also were with Jesus," she said to him.

But Peter denied it, saying, "Woman, I do not know him!"

Not long afterward another maid saw Peter and said, "You belong to them." Peter denied again that he was one of the disciples. And when a third person said he surely was one, because he talked like a Galilean, Peter began to curse and swear that he was not.

Then Jesus turned and looked out into the court where Peter was. At that moment a cock began to crow. Peter remembered the words that Jesus had spoken in the upper room, "Before the cock crows, you will deny me three times." And he turned and rushed out into the darkness, weeping bitterly.

The members of the Sanhedrin questioned Jesus and accused him. They had witnesses by whom they tried to prove that he was guilty of one thing and another, but the witnesses could not agree. The men who sat in judgment grew more and more angry and impatient because nothing was being proved. Then the high priest, whose name was Caiaphas, turned to Jesus and questioned him.

"Are you the Christ?" he asked. "Tell us."

Jesus answered, "If I tell you, you will not believe. . . . But from now on the Son of Man shall sit at the right hand of the power of God."

"Are you the Son of God, then?" Caiaphas demanded.

"You say I am," said Jesus.

Then the high priest took hold of his own robes and tore them in his anger. "That is blasphemy!" he cried. "There is no need of further witnesses."

And they all said that Jesus should be put to death.

CHAPTER NINE

"Behold Your King!"

Early the next morning Caiaphas and the other priests and rulers took Jesus to Pontius Pilate, the Roman governor.

Pilate's palace was in the city of Caesarea, but each year he came up to Jerusalem for the week of Passover. He brought a guard of Roman soldiers to make sure that no disorder should break out among the crowds who were gathered there. His headquarters were in a palace on the hill overlooking the Temple. It was here that the priests brought Jesus. Many people followed them. Perhaps the traders whom Jesus had driven out of the Temple were there, and others who had turned against him.

The crowd poured into the court of Pilate's house, and the priests sent in word that they wanted to see the governor.

Pilate came out on a balcony. He saw that the priests had a prisoner. He looked at Jesus.

"What charge do you bring against this man?" he asked of Caiaphas and the rest.

This question made them angry. "If this man has not done wrong we would not have brought him here," they answered.

"Take him yourselves and deal with him," Pilate told them.

This made the priests and the others even angrier. They said that they wanted Jesus put to death, but that the Roman law did not give them power to order that. Only Pilate could do so, and now they wanted him to act.

Pilate took Jesus alone and questioned him. He had heard that Jesus had been called King of the Jews, but he could not make any sense out of that. The only kingdoms he knew anything about were kingdoms that were made by armies. The Jews could not have a king of their own, because they were under Roman rule.

"Are you the King of the Jews?" Pilate asked Jesus.

Jesus answered, "You have said so." Then he told Pilate that his kingdom was a kingdom of love and not like the kingdoms of this world.

Pilate took Jesus back to the open court where the crowd was waiting.

"I do not find any wrong in him," Pilate said.

But the crowd would not hear of letting Jesus go. They shouted, "He has stirred up the people, all the way from Galilee to Jerusalem."

Pilate caught that one word — Galilee. Very well, if Jesus came from Galilee, let Herod decide what should be done with him. Herod was the ruler of Galilee, and it happened that he was in Jerusalem at that time. So to Herod Jesus was sent.

But when Herod questioned him, Jesus did not answer a single word. He had respect for Pilate, the Roman governor, but none for this wretched ruler who had put John the Baptist to death. Jesus simply stood there and looked at him. At last Herod could not endure his gaze any longer, and he sent Jesus back to Pilate.

Then Pilate tried again to set Jesus free. He reminded the crowd of a custom that at the time of Passover the governor would release one prisoner. Here was Jesus, who had been called King of the Jews. As a favor to them, Pilate would release Jesus.

But the crowd shouted that they would not have it. They did not want Jesus to be set free. Instead, they cried out to Pilate to release Barabbas — Barabbas, who had been arrested as a robber.

"Then what shall I do with Jesus, who is called Christ?" asked Pilate.

And they all shouted, "Let him be crucified!"

Then Pilate had Jesus beaten by the Roman soldiers, with whips of short leather thongs tipped with lead. And because the soldiers had heard that he was called a king, they mocked him, saying, "Hail, King of the Jews!" They twisted a crown from twigs of the thornbush and put it on his head, and they threw an old purple robe around his shoulders.

Pilate led out Jesus, wounded and bleeding from the beating, where the crowd could see him. "Look at him!" he said.

Pilate thought that this punishment would satisfy the people, but they kept shouting, "Crucify him! Crucify him!"

"I find nothing wrong with him," Pilate insisted. And he said again, "I will let him go."

"Crucify him!" the people shouted even more furiously than before.

"Behold your king!" said Pilate. "Shall I crucify your king?"

"We have no king but Caesar!" they cried. "This man has pretended to be a king. If you let him go, you are no friend of Caesar."

Pilate knew that he was in a trap. He might lose his place as governor if the priests sent word to Rome that Jesus had been called a king and Pilate had set him free. So Pilate, although he hated the priests, saw that they had won. He sent for a basin of water and he washed his hands to try to show that he was not to blame for Jesus' death. Then he handed Jesus over to the priests and the crowd to be crucified.

The enemies of Jesus among his own people had succeeded in having Pilate order what they wanted. But according to Roman law they could not themselves carry out those orders. Roman soldiers, with a centurion in command, now took charge.

They made ready the two beams which were to form a cross, and they laid these on Jesus' shoulders. Through the streets of the city he carried them, to a hill outside the walls, called Calvary. The crowd that had been in Pilate's court followed him. People poured out of the houses along the way to see what was happening.

The weight of the beams grew too heavy for Jesus to bear alone. The soldiers ordered a man named Simon, who had just come in from the country, to help.

When they came to the hill, the soldiers fastened the shorter beam over the other to form a cross. Then they stretched Jesus on it, nailed his hands and feet to the wood, and set the cross upright.

On each side of Jesus they set up another cross. On these they crucified two other men, both of them thieves.

The soldiers sat down around the foot of the cross and began to gamble for the clothes that Jesus had worn. Those who were close to Jesus heard him say, "Father, forgive them, for they know not what they do."

Outside the space around the cross, which the soldiers guarded, the crowd milled about. At Pilate's orders, a sign had been written and nailed up at the top of the cross, "This is Jesus, the King of the Jews." This enraged some of the crowd. This was no king of theirs! They began to shout to Jesus that if he could do all that he had said he could, then let him come down from the cross. And the priests wagged their heads and said, "He saved others; he cannot save himself. If he is the Christ, let him come down from the cross."

The thief on one of the other crosses also began to jeer at him. "You are the Christ, are you!" he said. "Then why don't you save yourself and us?"

But the second thief was different. Even there on the cross, he could see something wonderful in Jesus. He turned toward Jesus and said, "Lord, remember me when you come into your kingdom."

And Jesus answered, "I tell you certainly that this day you shall be with me in Paradise."

The hours dragged on. About three o'clock in the afternoon, Jesus cried with a loud voice, "My God, my God, why hast thou forsaken me?" — words from the beginning of one of the great old Hebrew psalms.

Mary, the mother of Jesus, and John the disciple, stood near the foot of the cross. Jesus spoke to them. He said to his mother that now John should be her son, and he said to John that he should take his mother and let her be as though she were his own. The other disciples of Jesus were standing, terrified, a long way off.

All his life Jesus had lived for God. Now in his heroic dying, too, he would make men know the love of God that was in him.

At length Jesus said, "It is finished!" Then, a moment later, he whispered, "Father, into thy hands I commend my spirit." His head drooped forward, and he breathed out his last breath.

The Roman centurion who had been in charge of the crucifixion said, "Truly, this man was a son of God!"

There was a man named Joseph of Arimathea, who perhaps for a long time had wanted to be a follower of Jesus but had not quite dared to have it known. When the evening came and it was growing dark upon the hill, he went to Pilate and asked that he might have the body of Jesus. Pilate gave his permission, so Joseph took the body down from the cross and wrapped it in a linen cloth. He carried it to his garden and put it in a new tomb which was cut out of rock. Then he rolled a heavy stone across the opening.

Mary Magdalene and another woman who had loved and followed Jesus were with Joseph when the body of Jesus was laid to rest.

To the disciples, hidden somewhere in Jerusalem, that night seemed the darkest night they had ever known. It seemed to them that nothing was left of all they had believed in and desired.

But the crucifixion was not the end; it was only the beginning.

Two days afterward, before the day had fully dawned, Mary Magdalene and two other women went to lay sweet spices in the tomb of Jesus. As they went, they wondered how they could roll away the stone that was across the entrance, for it was very heavy. But when they came there, they found that the stone was rolled away. Looking in, they saw what they thought was a young man, clothed in a long white robe. And they were afraid.

"Do not be afraid," he said to them. "You are looking for Jesus of Nazareth. He is not here. He is risen." Then he told them to go and tell the other disciples, and especially Peter, that Jesus was risen, and that they should see him again, as he had promised. Trembling and astonished, the women ran to carry the message.

At first the disciples could not believe what the women told. Peter and John ran to the tomb. John, who was younger, outran Peter and reached the open tomb first. While he hesitated outside, Peter arrived and went in. Then the two of them saw that the tomb was empty, as the women had said, and they went away.

But Mary Magdalene was in the garden again. She stood near the tomb where Jesus' body had been, and she wept. Then in the shadows she seemed to see two angels, who said to her, "Woman, why are you weeping?"

She answered, "Because they have taken away my Lord, and I do not know where they have laid him."

When she had said that, she turned around and saw someone standing there. She thought it was the gardener, and she begged him to tell her where the body of Jesus might be. But the one to whom she was speaking said just one word. He spoke her name, "Mary."

When she heard that voice, Mary Magdalene knew that it was Jesus. Full of love and wonder, she would have knelt down and kissed his feet, but he told her not to touch him yet. Then joyfully she went back to the disciples and told them, "I have seen the Lord!"

On the evening of that day two men who had been followers of Jesus, though they were not among the closest twelve, were going out from Jerusalem to a village called Emmaus. They talked together of all that they had been hearing in Jerusalem, and of the message the women had brought of the empty tomb. They did not know what to think.

Along the shadowy road there came another figure. He joined them and walked at their side. He asked them what it was that they were saying to each other.

"Are you a stranger to Jerusalem that you have not heard what has been happening there?" they asked.

What did they mean? he asked them.

Then they told him about Jesus of Nazareth, and how he had come up to Jerusalem, and how the chief priests and the rulers had condemned him to death and had crucified him. They said that they themselves had hoped that instead of being crucified he would have been the Savior of Israel. They went on to tell him how some women of their company had gone early in the morning to the tomb where his body had been laid. These women had come back, saying they had seen a vision of angels who said that Jesus was alive. But they themselves had not seen him, and how could they be sure?

Then the one who was walking by them began to ask them if they did not remember what the prophets had foretold long ago. Did they not know that Christ had to suffer before he could be the Savior? Had they not understood what the sacred writings had told of how he must live and die?

While he was speaking, they reached Emmaus. The two travelers begged the stranger to stop with them there. "The day is almost over," they said. "Come into the house and stay with us." So he went in.

They sat down at the table together. Their companion took bread and blessed it and broke it and gave it to them. In that instant, it was as though their eyes were opened. As the light fell upon the face and hands of the one they had thought to be a stranger, they saw that he was Jesus. But in the moment that they recognized him, he vanished from their sight.

Then they asked themselves how it ever could have been that they had not known him before. "Did not our hearts beat fast there on the road," they said, "when he talked to us?" Quickly they hurried back to Jerusalem to tell the disciples how Jesus had appeared to them and how at last, as he broke the bread, they had known him.

In Jerusalem they found the eleven disciples gathered with other friends of Jesus. The two men from Emmaus began to tell what had happened to them, when suddenly, there in the room was Jesus.

"Peace be unto you," he said.

Some of the men were so startled that they shrank away.

"Why are you troubled?" Jesus asked. "Look at my hands and feet, and see that it is I." And he showed them the marks made by the nails on the cross.

On another day Jesus showed himself to Thomas, one of the disciples, who had not been there the first time. Thomas had said that he could never believe that Jesus was living unless he saw him for himself.

Jesus said, "Peace be with you."

And Thomas cried out, "My Lord and my God!"

But the place where Jesus and the disciples had known and loved one another first was Galilee.

The Gospel of John tells that Peter and the rest of the disciples went back to Galilee to fish, as they used to do. They fished all one night, and caught nothing. As the day dawned, they looked up, and there was someone standing on the shore. He asked them if they had caught anything, and they answered no.

"Drop the net on the right side of the boat," he said. When they dropped it and drew it up again, the net was full of fish.

John said to Peter, "It is the Lord!"

When Peter heard him say that, he was so excited that he snatched up his fisherman's coat and leaped out of the boat to get to shore. The other disciples rowed the boat in, dragging the net behind them.

When they came up on the beach, they found a fire burning there.

"Come; have breakfast," said Jesus. And while they were so full of wonder and of happiness that they could hardly speak, he handed them bread. And they cooked their fish over the fire, and ate.

When breakfast was finished, Jesus turned to Peter. He called him by the old name which was his before he began to be a disciple. "Simon, son of Jonas," he said, "do you love me more than these?"

Peter answered, "Yes, Lord, you know I love you."

Jesus said, "Feed my lambs."

Jesus repeated his question. "Simon, son of Jonas, do you love me?"

Again Peter answered, "Yes, Lord, you know I love you."

"Feed my sheep," said Jesus.

Then, for the third time, Jesus asked, "Simon, son of Jonas, do you love me?"

Peter was hurt that Jesus should ask him that three times. "Lord," he cried, "you know everything. You know that I do love you!"

Jesus told Peter then of hardships and sufferings that he would have to face because of being a disciple. He told Peter that whatever happened he should not lose courage, but fearlessly carry on his Master's work.

Peter looked at John, who was standing near. "Lord," he asked, "what shall this man do?"

Jesus told him that what might happen to John was not for Peter to ask about. "You follow me," he said.

Presently Peter and the others went back to Jerusalem. One day, on a hill outside the city, near Bethany, Jesus was in their midst. He lifted up his hands and blessed them. Then suddenly he vanished.

Filled with wonder, the disciples said that Jesus had gone back now to heaven.

(page 70)

THE SAMARITAN AND THE INNKEEPER

(page 75)   Lee

JESUS ENTERS JERUSALEM

CHAPTER TEN

Men Made Brave by Jesus

So the time had come when Jesus no longer walked with his disciples. Their eyes could not see his face and their ears could not hear his voice as they used to do. The body which they had known and looked at was not now on the earth.

Yet, in a wonderful new way, they were sure that Jesus was still with them. He was in their thoughts; his love was in their hearts. He had said to them that they were to go and be messengers of his gospel, in Jerusalem first, in all Judea, even in Samaria, and out to the farthest parts of the earth. Wherever they went, his strength and encouragement seemed to be at their side. Every day they remembered how he had lived with them. Now it was as though he were living in them. They were Jesus' men, and the spirit of Jesus was guiding them in what to think and what to do.

When the eleven disciples, with some others who had loved Jesus, met together in Jerusalem, they decided to choose another disciple to take Judas' place. They wanted to have the old number of twelve complete again. They asked God to guide their choice. There were two men they thought of especially, because both had been followers of Jesus from the beginning. Each one knew about Jesus and could tell the story of his life. From these two men, they chose the one named Matthias.

While they were all in Jerusalem, on the day of one of the great Jewish festivals called Pentecost, they were thinking again of Jesus and of the work which they must do for him. They were so filled with joy and gladness and with a great new power, that it was as if a mighty wind were blowing and fire were coming down from heaven like halos round their heads. Crowds of people were in Jerusalem for Pentecost, and many of them came to where the disciples were. Then Peter stood up and preached to them.

He reminded them that the prophets had told that the day was coming when the spirit of God would come upon men in such a way as it had never come before. Now, he said, this had happened because God had appointed the disciples to preach the gospel — the good news of Jesus Christ. Then Peter told them about Jesus and how, although he had been crucified, he had risen again and was living with God. If they would listen to the gospel, Peter said, they would be set free from all that was cowardly and mean in their own lives, and they, too, could be followers of Jesus.

Many of those who heard were baptized, and this was the beginning of the church of Jesus. All the first disciples were Jews, and they still went to worship just as they used to do in the Temple and in the synagogues. But now they and the men and women who wanted to learn about Jesus began to meet also in one another's houses. They listened to those who had known Jesus and they prayed and helped one another in every way they could. In memory of the last supper which Jesus had had with his disciples in the upper room the night before he was crucified, they broke bread together. That was the simple beginning of the service which all Christian churches have continued—the Holy Communion.

Among the disciples, the two who took the lead were Peter and John. This was the same Peter who had denied Jesus in the court of Caiaphas; yet he was not the same. When Jesus came back from death he made Peter know that he loved him still, and that he trusted him. This time Peter did not fail that trust. John was the same John, hotheaded and quick-tempered, who had wanted to call down fire to burn up the Samaritan village which would not welcome Jesus. Yet he, too, was different. As he had loved Jesus, so now he was learning to love everyone who was in trouble and needed help.

One day Peter and John were going up to the Temple at the time of worship. There at the Temple gate lay a lame beggar, holding out his hands for coins from the passers-by. When he saw Peter and John, he asked them to give him something. Peter stopped and looked at him.

"I have no silver and gold, but I give you what I have," said Peter. He remembered the many times he had seen Jesus heal the sick, and he believed that the love of Jesus would help him to heal, too. Peter said to the lame man, "In the name of Jesus Christ of Nazareth, rise up and walk!"

The lame beggar felt strength coming into his feet and ankles.

He leaped up and began to walk. He went into the Temple with Peter and John, dancing with joy and praising God, and all the people followed.

They flocked around Peter and John and the man who had been lame. Peter took this chance to preach. He told the people, just as he had done at Pentecost, how the rulers of the nation, through ignorance and through sin, had crucified Jesus. But, Peter said, Jesus was risen again and his Spirit could be with all men to bless them.

Peter had not been preaching long when the news of it was carried to the priests. They were angry that anyone should dare to preach about Jesus in the Temple which they controlled. They sent men to arrest Peter and John and to hold them prisoners until the next day, for by this time it was evening.

In the morning their council met with Caiaphas, the high priest, and old Annas, Caiaphas' father-in-law, who had been high priest before him. They were men in authority, and they could be cruel. Peter and John were brought in and ordered to stand up before them.

"Who gave you permission to do what you have done?" the high priests asked.

Peter did not hesitate. "Rulers of the people and elders," he said, "you ask us about what has been done to the lame beggar, and how he was cured of his lameness. Let it be known to all of you, and to all the people of Israel, that it is by the name of Jesus Christ of Nazareth, the one you crucified, and who has been raised by God from the dead, that this man has been made sound and strong." And he told them that they could not be saved, and their nation could not be saved, unless they were ready to learn what Jesus had taught.

The old men of the council looked at Peter and John angrily. Who were these ignorant fishermen to dare to teach them? How had they become so bold? There could be only one answer. Peter and John had been with Jesus, and it was the spirit of Jesus which made them steady and unafraid.

All this time there, before the eyes of the rulers, stood the beggar who had been lame and now was healed. What could they say against that? What could they do when hundreds of people in Jerusalem had seen and admired what Peter and John had done? All the same, the rulers were determined to stop this kind of thing.

So once more they called Peter and John before the council and gave them orders that they should not preach in Jesus' name. But the two disciples of Jesus answered, "You must judge for yourselves whether it is right in the sight of God to pay more heed to you than to God. As for us, we cannot help but tell what we have seen and heard."

So the council of the rulers, when they had threatened Peter and John again, let them go, because they could not find any excuse for punishing them.

Peter and John went directly to join the little company of the followers of Jesus in Jerusalem. When they told the group what had happened, they sang hymns of praise to God and prayed together, and new gladness and courage from God came upon them all.

The disciples of Jesus had no church building, but they began to think of themselves as members of Christ's church. The book in the New Testament which is called the Acts of the Apostles tells of some of the happenings of those early days. It tells especially about the activities of Peter. People in Jerusalem began to believe that Peter had so much power that if even his shadow fell on them it would help them. So they brought the sick and laid them in the streets where he might be passing by.

It was told that once, when Peter went down to a town called Lydda, he saw a man named Aeneas who had the palsy and had been in bed eight years. Peter said to him, "Aeneas, Jesus Christ makes you well. Stand up, and put away your bed." And Aeneas did.

In the Book of Acts there is also the story of a woman named Dorcas, who lived in the city of Joppa. She was loved by all her neighbors because she was always doing kindnesses to everybody. Dorcas fell sick. Her friends who had nursed her laid her in her room as dead. They sent to Peter and begged him to come. When he arrived, he found a whole company of widows weeping. They told him of Dorcas' good deeds and showed him the clothes which she had made for the poor.

Peter put them aside. He went into Dorcas' room alone and kneeled down and prayed. Then he called her by her name, and said, "Rise!"

Dorcas opened her eyes. When she saw Peter, she sat up. He gave her his hand and lifted her up. Then he called her friends and gave her back to them, alive.

Peter had learned from Jesus to have pity on people in trouble and to want to help them. Now he was learning also to have no fear of those who had made themselves the enemies of Jesus.

Once, when Peter had been healing the sick in Jerusalem, the high priest and others of the ruling council heard of it. Angrily, they had Peter and some of the other disciples arrested and put into prison. The next morning they sent their officers to bring the prisoners for trial. But when the officers returned, they had an astonishing report. They said that they had gone to the prison and found the doors shut and the jailers in their places. But the prisoners were out in the Temple, teaching the people.

"Go and get them," the high priest said.

When Peter and the others stood before the council, the high priest asked them, "Did we not positively command you not to teach in the name of Jesus? And here you have filled this whole city with your teaching. You are trying to make us responsible for that man's blood."

But Peter answered, "We must obey God, rather than men." And he told the council again that Jesus, whom they had crucified, had been made by God the one Savior in whom Israel must believe.

The high priests and the other rulers were furious. But one of them, named Gamaliel, was wiser than the others. He wanted them to stop and think. He told the officers to send Peter and the other disciples out of the room. Then he began to talk to the men of the council. He reminded them of leaders who had risen up among the people and had pretended to be sent from God, and how one after another had come to nothing. That was the way it would always be, he said, with men who were not actually sent by God. The right thing to do was to wait and see.

As for Peter, and those who were with him, Gamaliel said, "Let these men alone. If what they are saying and doing is only man's work, it will come to nothing. But if it is of God, you cannot overthrow it. You might even find yourselves fighting against God."

The members of the council had no answer. So they called in the disciples. They had them beaten, told them again not to preach any more in the name of Jesus, and let them go.

Peter and the others went out rejoicing, not only because they were free, but because they had been able to stand up and take punishment for the sake of Jesus. And every day, in the Temple and in people's houses, they kept on preaching and teaching in his name.

The followers of Jesus helped one another, and especially they looked out for the poor. The twelve disciples who had been closest to Jesus when he was on earth were now called the apostles, for that word meant that they were the men whom he had especially named and sent out to tell of him. The apostles wanted to be sure that all those who were in need should be helped equally. It did not matter whether they were Jews or Gentiles (the name for all the different peoples who were not Jews) . The apostles said that they were so busy preaching and teaching that they did not have time to take care of dividing food. They suggested choosing seven men whom everybody knew to be honest and full of good sense and guided by the spirit of God, to take care of this business. The whole company agreed to this. So they chose seven men, who were to be called deacons, and brought them to the apostles. The apostles prayed, and laid their hands upon the heads of the seven, as a sign that they were being appointed now to this new work in the name of God.

The first man among these seven deacons was Stephen. He was not only the first one chosen, but it soon appeared that among them all he was the most eager and devoted. As he went about his work he told everyone of Jesus, and he healed those who were sick.

But there were people in Jerusalem who still clung to their stubborn dislike of Jesus and of everything connected with him. These people said that Jesus had not kept the Jewish law, and they contradicted Stephen whenever they heard him speak. They even bribed some men to swear falsely that they had heard Stephen speak blasphemy against the Jewish law and against Moses, the great lawgiver. So they stirred up a great commotion in Jerusalem and had Stephen arrested and brought before the ruling council.

Caiaphas had been the high priest when Jesus was crucified,

and it was certain that now he would be no friend to Stephen. Caiaphas wanted to know what the charge against Stephen was. The men who had brought Stephen said that they had heard him preach that Jesus of Nazareth would overthrow the Temple and that he would change the customs which had been handed down from Moses.

"Is all this so?" asked Caiaphas.

"Brethren and fathers, hear me," said Stephen. Then, with his face shining like the face of an angel, he began to recite to them their own history — the long and wonderful story of the people of Israel. He reminded them of Abraham and of Isaac and of Jacob; of Joseph sold into Egypt; of the children of Israel made slaves by Pharaoh; of Moses and of how he led the people out of Egypt and into the Promised Land; and of the stubbornness of the people when Moses tried to make them understand and obey the will of God. He told them that whenever prophets had arisen the people had resisted them and sometimes killed them. Now they, the priests and rulers, Stephen said, had done worse than the worst of all their fathers. They had taken the one to whom all the prophets had looked forward, Christ himself, and had put him to death upon a cross.

When the council members heard Stephen say that, they were so angry that they gritted their teeth. But Stephen, looking up to heaven, saw with wondering eyes a vision. "Behold," he said, "I see the heavens opened, and the Son of Man standing at the right hand of God!"

The crowd in the courtroom put their fingers in their ears to shut out Stephen's words. Then they broke into furious cries, rushed upon him, and dragged him through the streets and outside the city. There they picked up stones and hurled them on him. But as he was wounded more and more, Stephen prayed, "Lord, do not hold this sin against them." Then he said, "Lord

Jesus, receive my spirit." And when he had said those words, he died.

Standing at the edge of the crowd was a young man named Saul. It was at his feet that the angry people threw down their clothes when they were scrambling here and there to pick up stones. Even if Saul did not help to kill Stephen, he looked on and did not try to stop it.

For Saul hated the name of Jesus and everyone connected with him. Saul was there in Jerusalem, studying to become a teacher of the Jewish law. He thought, just as the priests did, that Jesus had been disobedient to that law. Now that Stephen had been killed, the first of Jesus' followers to die for his sake, it seemed to men like Saul that the time had come to get rid of all of the followers of Jesus. So wherever he heard of a house where any of them lived, Saul went to that house and arrested the men and women in it and carried them off to prison.

From that time some of the disciples of Jesus began to leave Jerusalem. But wherever they went, they preached of Jesus. A disciple named Philip went to the city of Samaria to preach there. He healed so many of the sick that there was excitement and joy among all the people. Now in Samaria there was a man named Simon. Up to this time he had had a great reputation for knowing the secrets of magic and witchcraft. All the people listened to him and were afraid of what they supposed to be his powers. When Simon saw the wonders of healing that were performed by Philip, he decided that he wanted to be like him. Simon asked Philip to baptize him, and then he stayed close by Philip, watching what he did.

Before long the apostles in Jerusalem heard of the work of Philip in Samaria, and they sent Peter and John to see what was happening there. When the two disciples met the people who had listened to Philip and who wanted now to follow Jesus, they laid their hands on their heads and prayed that the Holy Spirit of God might come upon them. Then, in answer to the prayers of Peter and John, joy and power in a wonderful new way did come to these new followers.

Simon noticed that immediately. If only he could do what Peter and John had done! So he went to them and offered them money if they would show him how he, by laying hands on people's heads, could make them different.

Peter looked at Simon with amazement. "You and your money perish together!" he exclaimed. "You seem to think the gift of God can be bought with money. You have no part in this matter, for your heart is not right with God. Repent of your wickedness, and pray God that your evil thought may be forgiven, for everything in you now is wrong."

Then Simon, being ashamed, begged Peter to pray to God for him.

Peter and John went back to Jerusalem, but Philip, after a time, went down toward the city of Gaza. As he walked along the road, he saw a man riding in a chariot. This man was a person of high rank under the queen of Ethiopia, and he had been to Jerusalem to worship. Now, on his way home, he was reading from the Book of the Prophet Isaiah. The Spirit of God speaking in Philip's heart told him to go and overtake the man in the chariot. So Philip ran after him. When he heard the stranger reading aloud to himself the words of Isaiah, Philip asked him whether he understood what he was reading.

"How can I," said the man, "unless someone guide me?" And he asked Philip to ride with him in his chariot.

The words of the prophet which the man had been reading were these: "As a sheep led to the slaughter, or a lamb before its shearer, is dumb, so he opens not his mouth. In his humiliation justice was denied him. . . . His life is taken from the earth."

"Tell me, I pray you," said the man from Ethiopia to Philip, "whom the prophet meant."

Then Philip told him about Jesus; of his life, and of his death, and of how in his courage and his gentleness he had come to be the Savior of the world. As they went along the road, they came to a place where there was water.

"Why can't I be baptized?" asked the man from Ethiopia.

"If you believe with all your heart, you can," said Philip.

"I believe that Jesus Christ is the Son of God," he said.

The two of them went together into the water, and Philip baptized the Ethiopian. Then Philip disappeared, but the man from Ethiopia went on his way rejoicing.

CHAPTER ELEVEN

Saul . . . and Simon Peter

After Stephen's death, Saul kept on hunting as hard as he could for the disciples of Jesus. When he found them, he carried them off to be punished. It may be that, as he saw their courage, he began to have different thoughts about Jesus, and about those who followed him. But he would not admit this yet, even to himself. He thought he would try to arrest all the followers of Jesus, not only in Jerusalem but in any other place where he might find them. So he went to the high priest and asked for letters to the chief men in the great city of Damascus.

Soon he was traveling on the road to Damascus. It was noontime. Suddenly it seemed to Saul that there blazed in the sky a light far brighter than the sun. He fell to the ground. Then he heard a voice saying, "Saul, Saul, why do you persecute me?"

"Who are you, Lord?" asked Saul.

And the answer came, "I am Jesus, whom you persecute."

Astonished and trembling, Saul whispered, "Lord, what shall I do?"

And the Lord said to him, "Rise, and go into Damascus, and there you will be told what to do."

The men with Saul were so amazed that they could not say a word, for they heard the voices, but they could not see anyone but Saul.

When Saul got up from the ground and started to walk, he found that he was blind. Men had to lead him by the hand into Damascus. For three days he could not see. All that time he did not eat or drink.

In Damascus there was a disciple of Jesus named Ananias. Ananias heard the voice of the Lord speaking to him in a dream. The voice said that he should go to a certain house on a street called Straight. There he should inquire for a man named Saul, who at that moment was praying.

Ananias was amazed. He said to the Lord that he had heard from many people of this man Saul. He had heard how much evil Saul had done to the disciples in Jerusalem. He had heard, too, that Saul was coming to Damascus with permission from the chief priests to arrest anyone who was a follower of Jesus. But the voice of the Lord answered Ananias that he was to do as he had been told. The voice said that Saul was to be a chosen servant of the Lord; that he was to carry the gospel everywhere, and would learn to suffer much for the sake of Jesus.

So Ananias obeyed. He found the house where Saul was, went in, and laid his hands upon the eyes that could not see. "Brother

Saul," he said, "the Lord Jesus, who appeared to you on the Damascus road, has sent me to give you back your sight, and to make you know that you shall be filled with the Holy Spirit."

Immediately Saul could see again. He rose up at once, and asked Ananias to baptize him.

Saul ate, and his strength came back. He stayed in Damascus, but instead of arresting the followers of Jesus, which everyone knew he had come to do, he went to the synagogues of the Jews and preached to them of Christ. They were all astonished. Most of them were angry at the way he had changed. They could not answer him, so they made up their minds to deal with him in another way. They would kill him.

Saul heard what they were planning to do. He could not go out any gate of the city, for all the gates were watched. So some followers of Jesus took him one night to a lonely place at the top of the city wall. There they let him down by ropes outside the wall. Then Saul was free to go back to Jerusalem.

When Saul reached Jerusalem, he wanted to join the group of Jesus' disciples. But nearly all of them were afraid of him. They could not believe that he had changed. They thought that if they let him join them, he would come as a spy.

But there was one man so big-hearted and generous in his belief that he trusted Saul. This man's name was Barnabas. Barnabas took Saul to the twelve apostles. He told them what had happened to Saul; how he had seen the vision of Jesus on the road to Damascus; how the voice of Jesus had spoken to him, and how after that Saul had preached boldly in Damascus in the name of Jesus. So Saul was received by the group in Jerusalem, and he began to preach in the synagogues there. But when it seemed that some of the Jews would kill Saul, the disciples took him down to the city of Caesarea on the seacoast and sent him by ship to Tarsus, which had been his home.

Up to this time, nearly all the disciples had come from among the Jews, but now begins a different story.

In the city of Caesarea there was a Roman centurion, named Cornelius. He had not been brought up in the religion of Israel but, like many other Gentiles, he respected the earnest way in which the Jewish people worshiped. He prayed to God himself and taught his family to pray, and he was generous and good.

One day as he was praying he thought he heard an angel call his name.

"Cornelius," said the angel. When Cornelius looked, he was afraid, and he said, "What is it, Lord?"

Then the angel told him that God had heard his prayers and seen the good deeds he had done. Now he was to send to the city of Joppa, and ask for a man named Simon. This man would tell him what he ought to do. Cornelius did not know it, but this Simon was Peter, Jesus' disciple, who had been preaching the gospel so bravely in Jerusalem.

Cornelius called two of his servants and one of his soldiers whom he trusted especially. He sent them to Joppa, which was about a day's journey away.

About noon the next day Peter went up on the flat roof of the house where he was staying, to be alone and to pray. While he was there, he grew hungry. Perhaps he was sleepy, too, for he dreamed that he saw something like a great sheet let down from the sky. In the sheet were all sorts of animals and birds, and he heard a voice saying to him, "Get up, Peter, and kill some of these to eat."

Peter was shocked at that idea. He had been trained all his life in the Jewish law which said that there were some sorts of animals and birds that no one ought to eat. These were called unclean. There were many of these unclean animals in the sheet let down from the sky.

(page 81) Coleman

THE LAST SUPPER

Coleman

THE RISEN CHRIST

"No, Lord," Peter answered. "I have never eaten anything common or unclean."

But the voice answered, "What God has cleansed, you must not call common."

Three times this happened. As Peter rubbed his eyes and wondered what this vision and the voice could mean, the three men from Cornelius knocked at the gate. They called out to ask whether a man named Simon was staying there. Peter understood that the Spirit of God was telling him to go with these men, no matter who they were.

He went down to the door and let the three men in. They told him that they had come from the Roman centurion, Cornelius, to inquire for a man named Simon.

"I am the one you are looking for," said Peter. "Why have you come?"

The men told him of Cornelius — that he was a good man, who loved God, and that he had seen a vision of an angel who had told him to send to Joppa to find Peter. Peter invited the men to stay with him until the next day, and then they all set out for Caesarea.

When they arrived at Cornelius' house, Cornelius went to meet Peter at the door. He kneeled at Peter's feet. But Peter said, "Stand up! I am only a man like you."

As he looked around, Peter saw that Cornelius had already brought together his family and his friends and neighbors. They were there to welcome him and to listen to whatever he might say.

Suddenly Peter understood what his dream had meant. He said, "You know that we Jews are forbidden by our law to be friendly with anyone of another nation or even to come into his house. But God has shown me that I am not to call any man common or unclean. So, when I was sent for, I came without making any objection. Tell me, then, why you sent for me."

Cornelius told Peter how the angel had commanded him to send to Joppa and ask Peter to come to Caesarea. "So I sent for you," the centurion said, "and it is good that you have come. Now we are all here in God's sight, to hear whatever God may command you to say."

Then Peter answered, "Surely I see now that God does not make a difference between one person and another, but that in every nation he accepts any man who loves him and does right." Then he told the company about Jesus, how he had gone about doing good, healing the sick and changing people who had been sinners; how he had been crucified, and then on the third day had been raised from the dead and had appeared to those who loved him. And Peter told them that he and the other disciples had been commanded to preach that Jesus would be the judge of all men, and that those who believed in him would have their sins forgiven.

Cornelius and his family and friends listened to Peter with joy.

Peter turned to some Jews who had come with him from Joppa and asked, "Can anyone forbid that these should be baptized, since the Spirit of God has come upon them as surely as on us?" So Cornelius and all his household were baptized, and Peter stayed with them for a while.

But when Peter went back to Jerusalem, and the other disciples there heard what he had done, some of them objected. They said that he had done wrong to visit and to eat with people who did not belong to the religion of Israel. But Peter told again the whole story from the beginning: how he had seen the vision on the rooftop in Joppa of the unclean creatures, and had been told by a voice from God that he was not to call anything common or unclean; how the messengers from Cornelius had come and he had been commanded to go with them; how Cornelius and his friends had listened when he preached to them, and then had been eager to be baptized. He said he remembered then the words of Jesus, "John did indeed baptize with water, but you shall be baptized with the Holy Spirit." And since God had given to Cornelius and his household the same gift of the Spirit which had been given to the disciples, "Who am I," asked Peter, "that I should stand against God?"

When they heard that, the disciples could say no more. They wondered and praised God, saying, "So God has given the Gentiles a chance to repent and to have a new life."

Some of the disciples who had been scattered from Jerusalem after the stoning of Stephen went as far as the city of Antioch. There they preached about Jesus, and many people listened and began to believe in him.

The apostles in Jerusalem heard of this, and they sent Barnabas to Antioch. This was the same Barnabas who had welcomed Saul. He was a good man, and full of faith, and as he talked to the new followers of Jesus in Antioch, they were encouraged. Others began to come to hear about Jesus. Barnabas saw that a great many people in Antioch could be made followers of Jesus. He thought of Saul, and went to Tarsus and brought him back to Antioch. Barnabas and Saul taught the people together and brought a large number of men and women into the church of Jesus. And it was there in Antioch that the followers of Jesus for the first time were called Christians.

Meanwhile, there was trouble in Jerusalem. James, the brother of John, was arrested and put to death. Peter also was caught and put in prison. Many of the disciples gathered together at the house of Mary, the mother of a young disciple named John Mark, to pray for Peter. While they were praying, a knock came at the gate. A maid named Rhoda went to answer. When she recognized Peter's voice she was so excited that instead of letting him in she ran back to tell the others that Peter was there. They could not believe it. They thought he was still in prison. Peter kept on knocking. Then the disciples went and opened the gate. And there, to their astonishment and joy, they saw their friend Peter.

Peter motioned with his hand that they were not to make any noise. In a low voice he told them how by God's mercy the prison doors had been opened, and he had been set free. Then he left and went to another place.

When day came, there was a great stir among the soldiers over what had become of Peter. Herod, the king, who had been responsible for his arrest, was in a rage when he heard that Peter was free. He commanded that the keepers of the prison be killed. Not long after that Herod was seized with a dreadful illness and he died.

In spite of what Herod had tried to do, the church of Jesus was growing every day. The disciples in different cities were ready to help one another whenever they could. About this time there was a famine in Jerusalem. Many of the poor people there had hardly anything to eat, so the Christians in Antioch decided to send them food. They took up a collection, and appointed Barnabas and Saul to carry it to Jerusalem. When Barnabas and Saul came back, they brought with them the young man, John Mark, who was a cousin of Barnabas.

Now Antioch was one of the great cities of the Roman Empire. It was rich and beautiful and important. It might have seemed that Antioch was a good place for Barnabas and Saul to stay and work, and that the Christians in Antioch would want to keep them there. But the Spirit of God gave Barnabas and Saul a different message. The gospel of Jesus must be carried out into the wide world, and they were the men to do it. So the Christians in Antioch laid their hands on the heads of Barnabas and Saul in blessing, and sent them and John Mark on their way. They would spread the word of God everywhere, like the sower that Jesus described in his parable, who walks across the fields in the springtime sowing the seed that will grow into great harvests of grain.

The three men sailed to the island of Cyprus. There they preached in the synagogues of the Jews. Then they went on to Asia Minor, which is the part of Asia just north of the Mediterranean Sea. They landed at the city of Perga. John Mark turned back to Jerusalem from there, perhaps because he was afraid or discouraged or possibly because he was sick.

Barnabas and Saul went forward on their journey alone. But from this time on, the man who once had persecuted the Christians and then on the road to Damascus had been changed into a servant of Christ, was not called Saul any more. Now and always afterward he was named Paul.

CHAPTER TWELVE

Paul Goes into the West

Barnabas and Paul went on to Antioch in Pisidia, a city which had the same name as the one from which they had started. There, as in other cities which they visited, they went first into the Jewish synagogue. For in any synagogue they would find men and women who already knew of God and his commandments.

Paul was invited to speak. He began, "Men of Israel, and you that fear God, hear me." Then he told the story of the Jewish people from the time when Moses led them out of Egypt, through the days of King Saul, and of David who became king after Saul. He reminded them that David had been called "a man after

God's own heart." He told them that Jesus was a descendant of David, but greater than David had ever been. For God had sent Jesus to be the Savior. He told them about John the Baptist, and how John had said he was not the Christ, but that a greater one would come after him. That one was Jesus. Yet the rulers of the people had wickedly taken him and crucified him. But God had raised him up and, although David and the great ones of other years were dead, Jesus was alive forever. Through Jesus, said Paul, men could learn to live according to the will of God as they never could have learned by the law of Moses, and those who believed in Jesus would have their sins forgiven.

After the synagogue service some of those who listened followed Paul and Barnabas to hear more. And many of the Gentiles asked Paul to preach to them on the next Sabbath.

The next week such a crowd came together that it seemed as if the whole city must be there. Most of the Jews were angry that Paul was preaching to Gentiles, and they contradicted what he said. Then Paul and Barnabas knew the time had come to make a great decision. They said to the Jewish crowd that it was right that the gospel should first have been preached to the synagogues of Israel, but now that the Jews had refused to listen, the gospel must be carried to the Gentiles instead. Most of the people were glad when they heard that, but some of the members of the synagogue stirred up the rulers, and Paul and Barnabas were driven from the city.

They came next to Iconium, and went into the synagogue. There also the people were divided. Part of them sided with Paul and Barnabas, but more took sides against them. So they were driven out of this city as they had been driven out of Antioch.

After that, Paul and Barnabas came to Lystra. In Lystra Paul healed a crippled man who had never in his life walked. Most of the people in Lystra had been brought up to believe in the gods who were worshiped in Greece and Rome. These gods were supposed to live on the cloudy top of Mount Olympus and to come down sometimes to walk about on the earth.

When the people of Lystra saw Paul heal the lame man, they cried out, "The gods have come down, looking like men!" They said that Barnabas, who was a big man, must be Jupiter, and that Paul was Mercury. Then the priest of the temple of Jupiter came hurrying to arrange a sacrifice to worship Barnabas and Paul. But they ran among the people, telling them to stop. They said they were not gods, but ordinary men. The very reason they had come, they said, was to teach people to stop worshiping idols and imaginary gods, and to worship instead the true God.

The people quieted down. But soon they were stirred up in a different way. Men came from Antioch and from Iconium who wanted to get rid of Paul. This time the mob was roused to such an ugly temper that they dragged Paul outside the city and stoned him. When they left, they thought he was dead.

But Paul was not dead. At last he rose up, and presently he was able to go on to another city, Derbe.

From Derbe he and Barnabas might have gone home by a shorter way. But they remembered the men and women in the cities they had visited who had listened to them and had believed in the gospel of Jesus. So, no matter how dangerous it was to return to those places where they had been nearly killed, they went straight back through Lystra, Iconium, and Antioch. There they encouraged the Christians and urged them to keep faithful, even if they should have to go through much danger and suffering.

At length Paul and Barnabas reached the seacoast and sailed home to the great Antioch, where the church had prayed for them and sent them forth. They told the Christians there of all that had happened to them on their journey, and of how God had opened the way for the Gentiles to become believers.

Paul and Barnabas were glad to be in Antioch again. But before long a question came up which gave them trouble. Some men came from Judea, the part of the country in which Jerusalem was. They told the Christians at Antioch that they could not really be disciples of Jesus unless they were willing first to obey all the laws and customs of the Jews. That contradicted what Paul and Barnabas had been preaching. They believed that Jesus had come to be the Savior of all men, Gentiles as well as Jews. And they were sure that it was not necessary for Jesus' followers to be thinking of old rules all the time. The great thing was to remember Jesus and the love of God which had been shown in him, and be thankful for that love. Then the spirit of Jesus would come into the heart of every Christian. It would not bring obedience to old rules, but a new and better way of living.

Even if the men who had come from Judea were mistaken, they were very much in earnest. They could not imagine how it could be right to have different ideas from those which had been handed down for hundreds and hundreds of years. If people who had worshiped God had followed certain customs ever since the time of Moses, then they ought to go on following them. The men from Judea thought that Paul and Barnabas had no business teaching as they did. And so they told the Christians in Antioch.

There was confusion and difference of opinion. At last it was decided that Paul and Barnabas and some others should go to Jerusalem and talk over the question with the apostles there.

In Jerusalem, when Paul and Barnabas arrived, a council was called of all the leaders of the Christian church. Peter stood up and began to speak. He reminded them that he had been the one to baptize the first Gentile, Cornelius the centurion. He said that since God had given his Spirit in the same way to men of different nations, he had shown that he meant to make no difference among them. The Gentiles had never been accustomed to the Jewish laws — laws about what to eat and not to eat, about how to wear their clothes and wash their hands and such matters. The Jews themselves had not managed fully to obey these laws, Peter said. It was not right to make the Gentiles learn all this before they could begin to follow Jesus. It was the love of Jesus, and not the law of Moses, that they needed to understand.

When Peter had finished speaking, Paul and Barnabas spoke. They told of all that had happened when they had gone out to preach the gospel to the Gentiles.

The members of the council sat very still and listened.

Then James, the brother of Jesus, stood up. He wanted to help the council to agree. He referred to what Peter had said. He thought that Peter was right. He believed that it had been fore-told by the prophets long ago that Gentiles as well as Jews should be the people of God. So he said that they ought not to make it hard for the Gentiles to become followers of Jesus. Would it not be enough, he asked, if the Gentiles kept the very important laws — the laws on which all good men would agree? Why should they be bound by the little laws which had come down from other times? Of course they must not worship idols, and they must not do anything shameful. For the rest, they could leave it to the spirit of Jesus in their hearts to tell them what to do.

What James said satisfied them all, so the council sent two men with Paul and Barnabas to tell the church in Antioch what the council in Jerusalem had decided. The Christians there were glad to hear that the disagreement had been settled happily. Only a few men here and there still clung stubbornly to the old ideas.

Before long, Paul and Barnabas decided to visit the little new churches which they had started in Asia Minor and see how they were getting on. Barnabas wanted to take his cousin, John Mark, with them again, but Paul said no. He would not have a man who had failed them the first time. Barnabas insisted, but Paul would not agree. So Paul and Barnabas separated. Barnabas took Mark, and they sailed away to Cyprus.

Paul took with him Silas, one of the men who had come from Jerusalem. They went to Asia Minor to visit the Christians in the cities where Paul and Barnabas had been before. At Lystra a young man named Timothy joined them. He was to become one of Paul's dearest friends. When they had gone a long way, they came to a city on the seacoast, called Troas. There Paul had a vision of a man in Macedonia, which was a country across the sea, in Greece. The man was calling him to come over and help the people there.

By this time another companion was with them. It was the physician Luke, the man who later wrote the Book of the Acts of the Apostles.

When they had crossed to Macedonia, they came to the city of Philippi. There a woman named Lydia listened to Paul's preaching, and she and all her family were baptized.

One day as Paul was going off to pray, he met a young girl who every now and then would fall into a trance, and would begin to speak as though some spirit from another world were speaking through her. People thought she could tell their fortunes, and money was made by charging people for them. When she saw Paul and Silas, the girl cried out, "These men are servants of the most high God, and they have come to show us how to be saved!" She kept on doing that, until Paul turned and commanded that the wild spirit should come out of her. Then the girl was quiet and calm, like any other person. But when the men who had been making money from her fortune-telling saw that she would not fall into trances and tell fortunes any more, they were furious with Paul. They took Paul and Silas to the market place to appear before the officers of the city. They said that these two men were Jews, and that they had come to this city which belonged to the Roman Empire and had made a disturbance which was against the Roman law. The officers ordered Paul and Silas to be beaten and put into jail.

So there in jail they were. In the middle of the night they were saying their prayers and singing a hymn when suddenly there was a great earthquake. It rocked the walls of the prison and shook all the doors open. When the jailer awoke and saw the doors open, he drew his sword and was about to kill himself. He thought all the prisoners must have escaped, and that he would be held responsible and be punished. But Paul called out, "Do not harm yourself; we are all here."

The jailer got a light and came in, trembling. He fell down before Paul and Silas and he cried, "Sirs, what must I do to be saved?"

Paul told him that he should believe in the Lord Jesus Christ; and he explained to the jailer, and to his family, about Jesus. Then the jailer washed the wounds which Paul and Silas had received when they were beaten. He took them into his house and gave them food, and he and his family were baptized.

The next morning the city officers decided that enough had been done to Paul and Silas. They sent word to the jail that Paul and Silas should be freed. The jailer brought the word in to them. "Now," he said, "you may go in peace."

But Paul said no, that he was more of a person than anybody in Philippi had supposed. They had said he was a Jew, and that was true. But those who were citizens of the Roman Empire had special rights. When Paul had lived in Tarsus, the city where he was born, he was a Roman citizen. These officers in Philippi had taken him, a Roman citizen, and without any trial had beaten him and thrown him into prison. Did they think that now they could tell him just to slip out quietly? No! Let them come themselves to him and Silas, and escort them from the prison.

The officers were afraid when they heard that Paul was a Roman citizen, and they did exactly what Paul told them to do. They themselves came and opened the prison doors for Paul and Silas, and these two followers of Jesus went out and returned to Lydia's house.

Paul and Silas stayed in Philippi for some time. Many men and women there became Christians, and Paul loved them very much. After he left, he wrote them a letter which is in our New Testament now, and is called the Epistle to the Philippians. In that letter Paul said to his friends in Philippi, "I thank my God in all my remembrance of you." He reminded them of Jesus, who had come to earth as a servant to help everyone. Paul told the Philippians that, instead of ever quarreling among themselves as to which one might be greatest, they should try to be like Jesus. He said that he himself had given up a great deal for Jesus' sake, but he did not take any credit for that. He kept on trying to be faithful, in the hope that the Lord some day would count him worthy to come and live with him. And near the end of the letter he wrote: "Finally, brethren, whatever is true, whatever is honorable, whatever is just, whatever is pure, whatever is lovely, whatever is gracious, if there is any excellence, if there is anything worthy of praise, think about these things."

From Philippi Paul and Silas went to the city of Thessalonica. There, on three Sabbath days, Paul went into the synagogue and preached. Some believed and joined the Christian group. Most of these were Greeks. Some of the Jews stirred up the rough people of the town and raised an uproar. A mob gathered outside the house of Jason, where they thought Paul and Silas were. The mob broke into the house, but Paul and Silas were not there. Then the mob laid hold of Jason and of some others whom they thought were followers of Paul, and took them before the rulers of the city.

"These men who have turned the world upside down have come here also," they cried. They said that Jason and men like him ought to be punished, because instead of obeying only the Roman emperor they were saying that there was another king, Jesus.

So the friends of Paul and Silas sent them away to the next city, Berea. In Berea the congregation in the synagogue listened to Paul until some of the men who had been in the mob at Thessalonica came there. They turned the people of Berea against Paul. So Paul went on board a ship and sailed to Athens, while Silas and Timothy stayed a while longer in Berea.

In Athens Paul was troubled to see how many altars there were to strange gods. He preached in the synagogue and he met some Greeks who were so learned that they thought they knew everything worth knowing. They said that Paul was just a babbler. They invited him to come to the assembly called the Areopagus, where the people gathered to hear and to discuss any new idea. They thought that they would have a chance to laugh at him.

Paul stood there in the Areopagus and spoke to them. He told them that as he passed by he had noticed an altar with these words upon it: "To the unknown god." He had come, he said, to tell them of a God whom all men needed to know, and of Jesus whom God had sent, and who had been crucified, and then had risen from the dead.

When he spoke of rising from the dead, some of the people mocked him. Others waved their hands and said, "We may listen to you some other day." But because they did not really wish to learn, there was not much more that Paul could say. Athens was perhaps the only city Paul visited in which he was not able to start a church.

From Athens Paul went on to the great, busy city of Corinth. Corinth was a seaport, and like other cities where the ships come in, its streets were filled with sailors and all sorts of people from many parts of the earth. There was rough behavior and much wickedness. But Paul found, as Jesus had said, that bad people were sometimes more ready to listen to the word of God than more respectable people.

In Corinth Paul met a man named Aquila and his wife Priscilla. They had come there a short while before from Rome, because the Emperor Claudius had ordered all Jews to leave Rome. Paul went to stay with them, and he made his living by helping them with their work, which was sewing tents. He preached first in the synagogue, as he nearly always did. But when the congregation there would not listen any more, he went out to the Gentiles, and those who wanted to hear him met together for worship in the house of a man named Justus.

So a new Christian church began to grow. This church at Corinth became one of the most important of all the churches. In the New Testament are two letters which Paul wrote to the Corinthians. In those letters he speaks of two other letters which he had written, but which we now do not have.

In the first letter Paul was evidently remembering what had happened in Athens just before he went to Corinth. He had learned there that people who think they know a great deal, according to the wisdom of this world, may be the last people to want to hear about the kingdom of God. The gospel of Jesus who died on the cross seemed to them only foolishness. But Paul said that when he went to Corinth he determined to preach nothing except Jesus Christ crucified, for that was the wisdom of God and the power of God. And because some of the Corinthians had been wishing that they might have some showy way of helping the church, Paul told them that just to be loving to one another was greater than anything else they could say or do.

"If I speak in the tongues of men and of angels," he wrote, "but have not love, I am a noisy gong or a clanging cymbal. . . . Love is patient and kind; love is not jealous or boastful; it is not arrogant or rude. Love does not insist on its own way; it is not irritable or resentful; it does not rejoice at wrong, but rejoices in the right. Love bears all things, believes all things, hopes all things, endures all things. . . . Faith, hope, love abide, these three; but the greatest of these is love."

In the second letter to the Corinthians, Paul told what he had been through for the sake of Jesus. He said that he had been whipped five times and beaten three times. "Once I was stoned; three times I have been shipwrecked; a night and a day I have been adrift at sea; on frequent journeys, in dangers from rivers, danger from robbers . . . danger in the city, danger in the wilderness, danger at sea, danger from false brethren; in toil and hardship through many a sleepless night, in hunger and thirst, often without food, in cold and exposure."

But Paul told them he could bear anything and do everything he had to do, through Christ who strengthened him. And he said that those who followed in the way of Jesus were as men "unknown, and yet well known; . . . as sorrowful, yet always rejoicing; as poor; yet making many rich; as having nothing, and yet possessing everything."

All this was part of what Paul wrote to the Corinthians after he had left them. While he was with them he told them and taught them a great deal more. For he was in Corinth nearly a

(page 109) Coller

ON THE ROAD TO DAMASCUS

(pages 38, 117) Holberg

THE SOWER

year and a half. Silas and Timothy came down from Macedonia and joined him there.

Toward the end of his stay in Corinth, some of Paul's enemies seized him and took him before Gallio, the Roman governor. They accused him of preaching in ways contrary to the Jewish law. But Gallio had no patience with these men and drove them out of his judgment hall, and Paul went free.

Some time after this, Paul left Corinth by ship. He went to the city of Ephesus. The people there wanted him to stay a long time. Paul said that he could not stay then, but that he would come back. Then he set sail again and landed in Caesarea and went from there to Antioch. And so Paul's second missionary journey came to its end.

Looking back on all that he had been able to do, Paul might well have said the words he wrote in one of his letters to the Corinthians: "Thanks be to God who gives us the victory through our Lord Jesus Christ!"

CHAPTER THIRTEEN

Difficulties and Dangers

Paul was never the sort of man who would stop long to rest. So after a little while he started out again from Antioch. He went once more to the cities and churches in Asia Minor, the country to which he and Barnabas had gone on their first journey. He came at last to the great city of Ephesus at the far end of Asia Minor.

In Ephesus Paul found some people who had heard of the preaching of John the Baptist but had never heard of Jesus. After he had talked with them and taught them, they were baptized, with great joy.

Paul preached in the synagogue at Ephesus for about three months. Then the same thing happened which had often happened before. Some did not like what he said, and would not listen any more. So Paul went to the hall of a school which belonged to a man named Tyrannus. There he preached for two whole years, and crowds of people came to hear him.

Paul did more than preach. He was able also to heal the sick, as other disciples of Jesus had learned to do. There were some men in Ephesus who tried to make people think that they could work miracles too. They had secret words which they said over those who were sick, and they claimed that these words were magic spells which evil spirits had to obey. They watched Paul, but they did not understand that he was bringing to men the power of the love of God in Jesus. They thought that he must have some spell which was stronger than theirs.

One day the seven sons of a man named Sceva decided that they would try Paul's words. When they met a man who was out of his mind, and who they supposed was full of evil spirits, they commanded the evil spirits to come out of him "in the name of Jesus, the one Paul preaches."

But the man shouted, "I know Jesus, and I know Paul, but who are you?" And he sprang on them and beat them and tore their clothes off and drove them away.

More and more people came into the Christian church. That made others disturbed and angry. In Ephesus was one of the most magnificent temples in all the world, a temple built for the worship of the goddess Diana. In the temple was a great statue of the goddess, and hundreds of people earned their living by making and selling little silver images of the statue. Now that the number of Christians was growing, not so many people bought these images. The business of the silversmiths who had made the images fell off.

One of the silversmiths, a man named Demetrius, called together some of the others and made an excited speech. How could they make their living if people stopped buying the silver images? Here was this man Paul, preaching a gospel that declared there was no value in idols and in images. Not only were the silversmiths losing their trade, Demetrius said, but they were letting Paul insult the great goddess Diana and her temple, which was the glory of their city.

Demetrius stirred up the silversmiths and other people so much that they began to shout, "Great is Diana of the Ephesians!" and they filled the city with confusion. At first they could not find Paul, but they did find some friends of his, Gaius and Aristarchus and Alexander. They crowded around these friends, still shouting, "Great is Diana of the Ephesians!"

But one of the officials of Ephesus came and made the crowd listen to him. He said that of course everyone knew that the people of Ephesus worshiped the goddess Diana, and nobody could take away the glory of her temple. The people might not like Paul, but Paul had not done anything yet that was against the law. If Demetrius and the others thought that he had, then let them take him into court. As things were now, they were liable to be arrested themselves for stirring up a riot; and he ordered the crowd to go home.

Still the city was full of anger. Yet Paul was not frightened. He knew that he had many enemies in Ephesus. But he knew too that a great work was there for him to do, and that he must stay and do it. So he did.

After a time, however, he felt that he ought to go to Greece. He crossed over to Macedonia to visit again the churches there, and then he went down once more to Corinth.

About three months later he returned to Asia Minor, and landed at the city of Troas. On Sunday Paul met and had supper with the Christians there. The next day Luke and some of the other disciples who were with Paul sailed from Troas to the city of Assos. Paul went by land and joined them. Then, all together, they took a ship to Miletus, which was not far from Ephesus. Some of the leaders of the church in Ephesus came down to the ship to meet Paul.

When they were all together, Paul talked with them lovingly of the days when he had been with them in Ephesus. He reminded them of the gospel he had preached, and of how he had tried to leave nothing undone to help them understand the love of God and the new life that had come to them through the Lord Jesus.

Now, Paul said, he must go to Jerusalem. He did not know exactly what would happen to him there, but something made him certain that dangers and sufferings lay ahead. "But none of these things move me," he said, "and neither do I count my life precious to myself. All that I want is that I may go on to the end with joy, and finish my work which the Lord Jesus gave me to do."

He said he was sure that they would never see his face again, and so now he wanted to give them his last message. He told them that as leaders of the church they should watch over the members like shepherds watching their flock of sheep. It was certain, he said, that in the time to come wrongheaded and wicked persons would come among them like wolves among sheep. He said he had tried to give them an example of not thinking of himself but rather of helping others.

"And now, brethren," he said, "I commend you to God; . . . I have showed you how in all things you must help the weak, and remember the words of the Lord Jesus that 'it is more blessed to give than to receive.' "

When Paul had finished, they all kneeled down and prayed

together. The men from Ephesus threw their arms about him and kissed him and wept, grieving most of all because he had said that they would not see his face again. Then they went with him to the ship, and the ship sailed out of the harbor.

Paul was starting on his way to new dangers.

It was a long voyage from Miletus, and several times Paul and his companions came into a seaport where they had to change to another ship. One of the cities where the ship stopped to unload her cargo was Tyre. There a little group of Christians met Paul and did their best to persuade him not to go on to Jerusalem. When he told them he must go, they brought their families to the shore and all kneeled down and prayed.

It was the same way at the place where Paul landed finally— the city of Caesarea. There he went to stay at the house of Philip, who was called the evangelist, because he was a preacher of the gospel.

While Paul was at Philip's house a man named Agabus came from a distance to see him. Agabus believed that God sometimes made him know beforehand things that were going to happen. He had a message now which he must give to Paul. He said he would give it not only in words but by a sign that everyone could see. So he took the belt Paul wore, and he fastened his own hands and feet with it. He said that this was what men who were waiting in Jerusalem would do to Paul.

Then all the disciples in Caesarea begged Paul not to go on to Jerusalem. But Paul answered, "Why do you weep and break my heart? I am ready not only to be bound and imprisoned, but also to die at Jerusalem, for the name of the Lord Jesus."

When they saw that he would not be held back, they stopped

trying to persuade him. They said, "The will of the Lord be done."

So Paul and his companions went by road to Jerusalem. There he saw James and the other leaders of the church. He talked with them and told them of all that had happened in his preaching to the Gentiles.

They were glad to hear his story. Yet some of them were a little troubled too. They knew that a good many of the Christians who had been born as Jews still clung to the old idea that the Jewish laws must be fully kept. Such people were suspicious of Paul because he had been preaching that the Gentiles did not have to follow the Jewish ways. James said that these men thought that Paul was trying to persuade even the Jewish Christians not to follow the old laws; that he encouraged them to forget everything their fathers had believed, which they had been taught since they were little children. Of course that was not true.

What Paul had been preaching was that different people of different nations might all come together into the church of Jesus. The Gentiles would not be obliged to follow rules of which they had never heard and which they did not understand, and the Jews would keep the customs which were familiar and dear to them.

James said that he knew what Paul meant, but that others did not. He asked Paul to do something special to change their wrong opinion. There were four Jewish Christians, he said, who still worshiped at the Temple. Would Paul go with them and take part with them in their worship, so that everyone could see that Paul himself still respected the old customs in which he had been brought up?

Paul said yes, he would do this. So he went to the Temple, and for a week he worshiped there.

In Jerusalem at that time were some Jews who were not Christians, who had come from some of the cities in Asia Minor where Paul had preached, and where the mobs had rioted against him. When they saw Paul in the Temple, they said that he had come there to insult it. They said also that he had brought a Gentile into a part of the Temple which was holy, and where no one but a faithful Jew was ever allowed to enter. It was not so, but they said it was, and they made such a noise and fury that soon an angry crowd had gathered. The mob dragged Paul out of the Temple and were about to kill him.

A report of this was carried quickly to the commander of the Roman troops on guard in Jerusalem. He immediately went with several centurions and their companies of soldiers to the Temple. When the crowd saw the Roman commander and his troops, they stopped beating Paul. But the Roman commander ordered chains to be put on him, and he roughly demanded to know who Paul was and what he had done. The people shouted, some saying one thing and some another. When the Roman commander could not make out from all the yelling and confusion what the trouble was, he ordered that Paul should be taken into the castle. The soldiers had to force their way with Paul through the mob. All the while the crowd shouted, "Get rid of him!"

As they came near the castle, Paul said to the commander, "May I say something to you?"

"What! Can you speak Greek?" the commander asked. For Greek was the language that was understood by many different people in the Roman Empire. "I thought you were an Egyptian — the one who a while ago stirred up a revolt."

"No," said Paul, "I am a Jew, a citizen of Tarsus, which is no mean city. I beg you, let me speak to the people."

The Roman gave him permission, and Paul stood on the stairs

and motioned with his hand for silence. When the crowd grew still, he began to speak to them in Hebrew: "Brethren and fathers," he said, "hear the defense which I now make to you."

And when the crowd heard him speaking in Hebrew, they grew quiet.

"I am a Jew," Paul went on, "born in Tarsus, but brought up in this city, a pupil of Gamaliel, and taught perfectly according to the way of the law of our fathers, and full of desire to work for God, as you are today.

"I persecuted the Christians to the point of death. I seized both men and women and carried them off to prison. The high priest and all the elders will bear witness to this, for I had letters from them to their friends in Damascus, and I went there to arrest the disciples of Jesus and bring them to Jerusalem to be punished.

"Then, as I was on the road to Damascus, suddenly about noon a great light from heaven shone around me. As I fell to the ground, I heard a voice that said to me, 'Saul, Saul, why do you persecute me?' I answered, 'Who are you, Lord?' And he said, 'I am Jesus of Nazareth, whom you persecute.'

"Those who were with me saw the light, but they did not hear the voice of the one who was speaking.

"I said, 'What shall I do, Lord?' and the Lord said to me, 'Rise, and go into Damascus. There you shall be told of all that you are to do.'

"When I could not see because of the brightness of the light, I was led by the hand into Damascus. And there a man named Ananias, one who kept the law and was held in high respect by all the Jews who lived there, came to me. He said, 'Brother Saul, receive your sight.' At that moment I could see. He said to me, 'The God of our fathers has chosen you to know his will, and that you should see Jesus, and hear his voice; for you will be a witness for him to all men of what you have seen and heard. And now why do you wait? Rise, and be baptized.'

"Then when I came back to Jerusalem, I was praying in the Temple, and I fell into a trance. I saw Jesus, and he said to me, 'Make haste, and get out of Jerusalem quickly, for they will not listen to you here.' And I said, 'Yes, Lord, they know that I carried off to prison and beat all those who believed in you. And when Stephen died for you, I stood by and consented to his death.' And Jesus said, 'Depart; for I will send you far away, to the Gentiles.' "

When they heard the word Gentiles, the crowd began to yell again, "Away with such a fellow! He is not fit to live." And they tore their clothes and threw dust into the air.

The Roman commander then ordered that Paul should be taken into the castle and whipped until they found out what he had done to make the crowd shout so against him.

But when Paul had been bound, he said to the centurion in charge, "Does the law give you the right to whip a man who is a Roman citizen, and has not been condemned?"

When the centurion heard that, he went and said to the commander, "This man is a Roman."

Then the commander came and asked Paul, "Tell me, are you a Roman citizen?"

And Paul answered, "Yes."

The commander said, "It cost me much money to become a Roman citizen."

"But I was born one," said Paul.

The commander was uneasy then because of the way Paul had been treated, and he took the chains off him. The next morning he commanded the chief priests and all their council to appear, and he brought Paul and set him before them. And again Paul made his defense.

There was a division of opinion in the council. Some of the Pharisees said, "We find no evil in this man; and if a spirit or an angel has spoken to him, let us not fight against God." So the council broke up in fierce disagreement. The Roman commander, fearing that Paul might be torn in pieces between the two quarreling sides, took him back into the castle.

After all that had happened Paul might easily have been discouraged. Instead, the next night he heard the Lord Jesus say, "Be of good cheer, Paul, for as you have spoken for me in Jerusalem, so you shall speak for me also in Rome."

CHAPTER FOURTEEN

Paul Before the Governor

There were some men who had made up their minds that they would not let Paul get to Rome or anywhere else alive, if they could help it. More than forty of them had vowed that they would neither eat nor drink until they had killed Paul. They went to the chief priests and elders and told them of their vow. This was the plot they laid: The council was to ask the Roman commanding officer to send Paul to them the next day, as though they wanted to examine him again, and while Paul was being taken there, the forty men would have their chance to kill him.

It happened, though, that the son of one of Paul's sisters lived

in Jerusalem. This nephew of Paul heard what the forty men
were plotting. He got into the castle and told Paul. Paul sent
for one of the centurions and said, "Take this young man to the
commanding officer, for he has something to tell him."

The centurion did as Paul asked, and said to the commander,
"Paul, the prisoner, called me and asked me to bring this young
man to you, for he has something to say."

Then the commander took Paul's nephew aside and asked
him, "What is it you have to tell me?"

The young man answered, "Some of the Jews have agreed to
ask you to bring Paul down tomorrow to the council as though it
wanted to examine him again. But do not consent! More than
forty men lie in wait for him; men who have vowed that they
will neither eat nor drink until they have killed Paul. Now they
are all ready. They need only for you to let Paul come."

The commanding officer sent the young man away, asking
him not to tell anyone that they had spoken together. Then he
called two centurions and said to them, "Get two hundred
soldiers ready to go to Caesarea, with seventy horsemen and two
hundred spearmen. Have them ready by the third hour of the
night, and have a horse for Paul to ride; and see to it that he is
brought safely to Felix, the governor."

And he wrote a letter for the centurion to carry:

"Claudius Lysias, to his excellency the governor Felix, greet-
ing:

"This man was seized by the Jews, and was about to be killed
by them, when I came upon them with the soldiers and rescued
him, having learned that he was a Roman citizen. And desiring
to know the charge on which they accused him, I brought him
down to their council. I found that he was accused about questions of their law, but charged with nothing deserving death or
imprisonment. And when it was shown to me that there was

a plot against the man, I sent him to you at once, ordering his accusers to state before you what they have against him."

So the centurion and the soldiers took Paul that night as far as a town called Antipatris, and the next morning the seventy horsemen went on with him as his guard, while the others went back to Jerusalem. When the centurion had come to Caesarea, he gave the letter to the governor and brought Paul before him. After the governor had read the letter, he asked Paul what province of the Empire he had lived in. Paul told him, Cilicia.

"I will listen to you when your accusers come," the governor said. And he ordered that Paul should be held in the castle room kept for prisoners.

Five days later the high priest arrived, with others of the council, and with a lawyer named Tertullus, who was to make the charge against Paul.

Tertullus began by flattering the governor. "Because of you," he said, "we have enjoyed quiet times, and through your kindness much good has been done to our nation, and always and everywhere we thank you for this, most noble Felix. However, I pray you that in your goodness you will listen to us. I will be brief."

Then, pointing at Paul, he went on: "We have found this man a wretched nuisance, a fellow who has stirred up trouble among the Jews through the whole world. He is a ringleader of the followers of Jesus. When he was going into the Temple, we took him and intended to judge him according to our law. But your officer took him out of our hands. By examining this man yourself, you can understand the charges we bring against him."

The others who had come with Tertullus declared that what he had said was true.

The governor told Paul that now he could speak.

Paul said, "I do the more cheerfully answer for myself because I know that you have been for many years a judge of this nation."

Then he went on to tell what had actually happened in Jerusalem, and to deny that he had done any wrong. He told how some of the Jews who had come from other countries to Jerusalem had stirred up the riot in the Temple, without any good reason. He said that the men who had tried to kill him were the ones who ought to be here before the governor.

Felix decided that he would have to hear more about this matter. He said he would wait until Claudius Lysias came down to Caesarea, and then he would continue the trial. He ordered the centurion to keep Paul, but not to shut him in prison, and to let his friends come in to see him.

Now the wife of Felix was a Jewess. A few days later Felix sent for Paul, and he and his wife listened while Paul told them about Christ. And as Paul spoke about right living and self-control and the judgment to come, Felix was alarmed. "Go away for now," he said to Paul. "When I have a convenient time, I will send for you again."

But all the while he was thinking too that perhaps Paul would offer money to be freed; and every now and then Felix would send for him, to see what Paul might say.

Two years went by, as Felix let the whole matter drag along. Then he got word from Rome that another man, Porcius Festus, had been appointed governor in his place. He decided that as his last act he would do the Jews a favor, and so when he moved out of Caesarea, he left Paul in chains.

When Porcius Festus, the new governor, arrived, he went up from Caesarea to Jerusalem. There the high priest and others of the council lost no time in complaining to him against Paul. They tried to persuade Festus to have Paul sent to Jerusalem. There was still the same plot that had been made before — to kill Paul on the road. But Festus answered that he intended to keep Paul in Caesarea. If any of them wanted to accuse Paul, they would have to come down there to do it.

In about ten days Festus himself went back to Caesarea, and some of the priests and others from Jerusalem followed him. Paul was brought again into the judgment hall, and once more the Jewish leaders brought their angry charges against him. Festus, like Felix, was willing to do them a favor, and so he asked Paul whether he would consent to go up to Jerusalem and be tried there.

Paul answered that, according to the Roman law which the governor well knew, he could not be handed over to the Jewish rulers unless some crime had been proved against him, and none had been or could be. "I stand," Paul said, "at Caesar's judgment seat. I appeal to Caesar."

By those words he meant that the governor's court represented the emperor of Rome, and he asked now that his case be tried by the emperor himself.

Festus spoke for a moment with those around him. "You have appealed to Caesar," he said to Paul. "To Caesar you shall go."

Because Paul had appealed his case to Caesar, he had to be sent to the emperor's court in Rome. Before Festus could arrange to have him taken there, Festus had a visit from Herod Agrippa, whom the Romans had allowed to act as ruler of a part of Palestine. Herod's wife, Bernice, was with him.

Festus said to Herod, "There is a man here who was left in prison by Felix. The chief priests and elders of the Jews informed me about him, and wanted me to condemn him. But I answered them that it is not the Roman custom to hand any man over to be put to death until he can have his accusers face to face before him and a chance to answer for himself. So, when his accusers did come here, I sat at once on the seat of judgment and ordered the man to be brought in. But when the charges against him were set forth, I found that he was not being accused of any

(page 119)   Coller

PAUL AND BARNABAS AT LYSTRA

Coller

PAUL IN PRISON

such matters as I had supposed. Instead, it seemed to be a question as to some of their Jewish superstitions, and especially in regard to one Jesus, who was dead, but whom this man Paul has declared to be alive. And because I had no clear idea about such questions, I asked Paul whether he would go to Jerusalem and be tried there. But Paul appealed for a hearing before the emperor, and so I ordered him to be kept until I could send him to Rome."

Herod said, "I should like to hear the man myself."

"Tomorrow," said Festus, "you shall."

So, on the next day, Herod and Bernice were ushered with pomp and ceremony into the great hall. The chief Roman officers and the important men of the city were there also. Then Paul was brought in.

Festus said, "King Agrippa, and all men who are here with us, you see this man whom the Jews brought before me, both at Jerusalem and here, crying out that he should not be allowed to live. But when I found that he had not done anything deserving death, and when he appealed to Caesar, I determined to send him on to Rome. But I have nothing certain to write the emperor. Therefore I have brought him in before all of you, and especially before you, King Agrippa, so that after this examination I may have something to write. It seems to me foolish to send a prisoner and not at the same time be able to state plainly the crime with which he is charged."

Then Agrippa said to Paul, "You have my permission to speak for yourself."

Paul stretched out his hand and answered, "I am happy, King Agrippa, that I can answer for myself before you today concerning the things of which the Jews have accused me. I know that you are expert in regard to Jewish customs and questions. So I beg you to hear me patiently.

"All the Jewish people know my manner of life since I was a young man in Jerusalem. If they would say the truth, they would tell you that I lived as a Pharisee, in the strictest manner of our religion. And now I stand here and am judged for the hope of the promise made by God to our fathers — the promise which our twelve tribes, who have served God day and night, have hoped for. It is for the sake of that hope, King Agrippa, that I am accused of the Jews.

"Why should it seem to you a thing not to be believed, that God should raise the dead?"

When Paul asked that, there was astonishment. Quickly he went on:

"I used to think myself that I ought to do everything I could against the name of Jesus of Nazareth, and that is what I did in Jerusalem. I shut up in prison many saintly men and women, when the chief priests had given me authority. When these people were condemned to death, I gave my vote against them. I punished them in every synagogue, and in my rage I even went to foreign cities to find them.

"As I journeyed to Damascus, with authority from the chief priests, at midday, O king, I saw on the road a light from heaven, brighter than the brightness of the sun. It shone about me and those who traveled with me. When we had fallen to the ground, I heard a voice speaking to me, and saying in Hebrew, 'Saul, Saul, why do you persecute me?'

"I said, 'Who are you, Lord?' And he said, 'I am Jesus, whom you persecute. But rise, and stand on your feet; for I have appeared to you to make you a witness for me. For I will send you to the Gentiles, to open their eyes and to turn them from darkness to the light, and from Satan to God; so that they may have forgiveness of sins, and become followers of me.' "

Paul's eyes were shining now. He looked at the king, and he

cried, "O King Agrippa, I was not disobedient to the heavenly vision! First to those who were in Damascus, then at Jerusalem and through all Judea, and then to the Gentiles, I preached to the people, begging them to repent and turn to God. That was why some of the Jews seized me in the Temple and tried to kill me. But I have had the help of God, and to this day I have kept on preaching what the prophets and Moses foretold — that Christ should suffer, and that he should be the first to rise from the dead, and that he should give light to his people and to the Gentiles."

When Paul said that, Festus exclaimed in a loud voice, "Paul, you have gone crazy! So much learning is making you lose your mind."

"No, I am not mad, most excellent Festus," Paul answered. "I speak only the truth, and speak it soberly. The king knows of these things. I am sure none of them has escaped his notice. What I have told of was not done in a corner."

Then he turned directly to the king. "King Agrippa," he said, "do you believe the prophets?" And when Agrippa did not answer, Paul went on, "I know that you do believe."

If Agrippa's heart was touched, he was ashamed to let others see it. He answered Paul, "In so short a time you think you can make me a Christian?"

Paul answered, "Whether short or long, I would to God that not only you but all who hear me today might become such as I am, except for these chains."

Then King Agrippa rose, and Festus and Bernice, and those who had been sitting with them, and left the hall. When they were outside, they talked together. They were the judges and Paul was the prisoner, but they were the ones who were uneasy now. Herod Agrippa was a Jew, so he knew the writings of the prophets who had promised in the name of God that a Savior would come. Paul had said that Jesus, who had died on the cross but had risen from the dead, was this promised Savior whom all men must obey.

Herod Agrippa was troubled by Paul's words. As for Festus, he doubted what Paul said, but he still was bothered about what to do with him. Festus and Herod Agrippa agreed that Paul had done nothing to deserve death or imprisonment.

And Agrippa said to Festus, "This man could have been set free, if he had not appealed to Caesar."

CHAPTER FIFTEEN

Over Stormy Seas to Rome

So Festus sent Paul on to Rome. He put him in charge of a centurion named Julius, who with his soldiers was to guard Paul and some other prisoners. At Caesarea they were taken on board a ship, which set sail and put out to sea.

The centurion was kind to Paul, and treated him with courtesy. When the ship put in at the port of Sidon, he let Paul visit friends of his who lived there.

At first the travelers had fair winds and a smooth sea, and all went well. But when they had sailed as far as the island of Cyprus, the wind turned against them and they went ahead slowly. With difficulty they reached a harbor called Fair Havens. By now it was late in the year and Paul, who had traveled this way before, knew that the season for rough winter weather was almost upon them. He told the centurion and the captain of the ship he was sure that if they kept on, they would run great risk, not only to the ship and her cargo but also to the lives of all on board. But the captain and the owner of the ship thought that Fair Havens was not a good place to anchor for the winter, and the centurion listened to the captain rather than to Paul.

So they started out again to sea. At first the winds were gentle. But before long a storm arose, and violent winds began to blow. The ship could not make headway, and was driven along helplessly. When it came under the shelter of a small island, the sailors did the best they could to strengthen the ship against the winds and seas. But the next day the storm was so fierce that the sailors began to throw the cargo overboard, to make the ship ride higher in the waves. The day after that they threw overboard all the spare parts of the ship itself. The food had almost given out. Day after day went by without a sight of either sun or stars. The storm raged, and the men on the ship gave up all hope of being saved.

Then Paul came forward and said, "Men, you should have listened to me. All the same, I tell you to take courage, for though we may lose the ship, there will be no loss of life. This very night there stood by me an angel of the God to whom I belong and whom I worship, and he said, 'Do not be afraid, Paul. You must stand before Caesar; and God has given you the lives of all the men who are sailing with you.' So take courage, men, for I have faith in God that it will turn out exactly as I have been told. But we shall have to run the ship on the shore of some island."

On the fourteenth night of the storm the ship was still drifting. About midnight the sailors thought they were nearing land.

They took soundings and found that the water under them was twenty fathoms deep. A little farther on, they dropped the measuring line again and found that the depth was only fifteen fathoms. They were afraid then that the ship might be blown onto the rocks, so they put out four anchors from the stern, and prayed for day to come.

Some of the sailors decided to try to escape from the ship. They lowered a lifeboat, pretending that they were putting out an anchor from the bow. Paul said to the centurion and to the soldiers, "Unless these men stay in the ship, you cannot be saved." So the soldiers cut the ropes of the boat the sailors had lowered, and it was swept away before the sailors could get into it.

Just before daybreak, Paul urged them all to take something to eat. "It will give you strength," he said. "Not one of you is going to be hurt." Then Paul took bread and gave thanks to God. As he began to eat, they began to eat also; and, feeling encouraged, they went to work again to lighten the ship. This time they threw out the wheat with which it was loaded.

At length day broke. They could see land, but they did not know what land it was. They saw a bay with a beach, and they determined to try to run the ship ashore. So they cut the anchors loose and left them in the sea, and straightened the rudder. With one sail hoisted into the wind, they headed for the beach. But with a great shock the ship struck a shoal, and the bow of it hung there. Huge waves, racing from behind, began to smash the stern.

The soldiers thought that they should kill the prisoners, so that none of them could swim off and escape. But the centurion, who wanted to save Paul, stopped them. He ordered all men who could swim to dive overboard and swim to land. The rest were to get there as best they could, on planks and other broken pieces of the ship.

And so it was that all of them — Paul, centurion and soldiers, captain and sailors — came safely to shore.

After they had landed, natives of the island, which they learned was Malta, came up to them. They welcomed the ship-wrecked men and kindled a fire for them, for it was raining and cold. Paul had collected a bundle of sticks to put on the fire. A poisonous snake crawled out of the sticks and wrapped itself around his hand. When the natives saw the snake hanging there, they said, "This man must be a murderer. He has escaped from the sea, but justice has caught up with him and will not let him live." But Paul shook the snake off into the fire and was not hurt. The natives stood and watched, expecting to see Paul fall down dead. When they had waited a long time and nothing happened to him, they changed their minds and said that he must be a god.

Near the place where they had come ashore lived Publius, the most important man of the island. He took Paul and his companions to his house. It happened that Publius' father lay sick with a dangerous illness. Paul went to his side and prayed, and laid his hands on him, and the sick man was healed. When this news was spread about, other sick people came, and Paul healed them also.

After three months the centurion was able to arrange for another ship to take Paul the rest of the way to Italy. They landed at a harbor not far from Rome, and were met by some of the Christians. Then they went along the Appian Way to the great city which was the capital of the world. There the centurion delivered his prisoners. Paul was allowed to stay by himself, with only one soldier to guard him.

Three days later Paul called together the leading men of the Jews who lived in Rome. He told them how he had been arrested in Jerusalem, and how he had appealed to the emperor, and of the voyage to Italy. He said he wanted them to know that he had done nothing against the religion of their fathers, in which they all believed. Instead, all that had happened to him had come about because he preached the hope of Israel.

These leaders of the Jews said, "We have received no letters about you, and no one who has come to Rome has told us anything bad of you. We should like to hear what your ideas are, though with regard to the Christian belief, we understand that everywhere it is spoken against."

They set a day when they would talk with him. On that day a great many of them came to Paul where he was lodging. From morning till evening he spoke to them of the kingdom of God, and tried to persuade them about Jesus, and to prove to them that what he told about him was according to what Moses and the prophets had foretold long ago.

Some were convinced by what Paul said; others would not believe. So, disagreeing among themselves, they turned to go away. As they were leaving, Paul spoke his final word. He repeated what the prophet Isaiah once had said: that sometimes when God's word is spoken to a people they shut their eyes so that they cannot see, and close their ears so that they cannot hear, and will not let God himself make them understand. So, said Paul, since those who once had been God's chosen people would not listen, the gospel would be given to the Gentiles, and they would hear.

Paul lived in Rome for the next two years. He welcomed all who came to him, and preached of the kingdom of God and of Jesus Christ.

With that, the Book of the Acts of the Apostles ends, but it is not the end of the story of Paul. Exactly what Caesar said and did when Paul's case was brought before him we do not know, but after a time Paul was freed. He seems to have gone again to Ephesus and to some of the other cities where he had worked and preached before. He wanted to go to Spain, and perhaps he did go there. But at length he was arrested again. This time, when he was brought to Rome, he was treated in a very different way. An evil emperor named Nero was on the throne. Paul was kept in prison, and he realized that now he would be put to death. Some of the letters he wrote show what he was thinking. Instead of being afraid or sad, he rejoiced that he was counted worthy to suffer for Christ's sake. To Timothy, the young companion whom he had loved so much, he wrote, "I have fought the good fight, I have finished the race, I have kept the faith."

Years before he had stood by and seen Stephen give up his life in the name of Jesus. Now he gave up his life too. When he died he could know, as he had written to Timothy, that "henceforth there is laid up for me a crown of glory."

CHAPTER SIXTEEN

The Holy City

Besides the Gospels, and the Acts of the Apostles, and the letters of Paul which have been already named, there are in the New Testament other letters of Paul. There are letters to the Galatians and to the Romans and one to Philemon, which is a beautiful short letter about a runaway slave. Two letters bear the name of Peter, and three the name of John. There are a few others. Last of all the books in the New Testament is the Book of Revelation.

This was written a long lifetime or more after Jesus had been crucified and had risen. As the years had gone by, the Roman

Empire had begun to persecute all Christians. In temples throughout the Empire, statues of the emperor were set up. Roman citizens were supposed to bow down before these statues, as though to worship the emperor like a god. The Christians would not do this, and so Christians were thought of as enemies of Rome.

By the time the Book of Revelation was written, so many Christians were being imprisoned and put to death that men began to think that the whole Christian church might be destroyed. Then a Christian by the name of John had a vision. He saw the throne of God in heaven, and the angels around it, and he saw the risen Jesus. In his vision he saw also wonderful, strange things, such as appear in dreams. He saw the judgment day, and Rome with all its pride and power destroyed, and those who had followed Jesus gathered around the throne of God.

John wrote his vision in a book, so that Christians who were being persecuted could believe that they, and not the cruel power of Rome, would win the victory. It was not safe for John to write in a way that Roman officials would understand. So in the Book of Revelation John called Rome, Babylon, but the Christians understood.

"Fallen, fallen, is Babylon the great!" he wrote.

"And the kings of the earth will weep and wail over her when they see the smoke of her burning; they will stand far off, in fear of her torment, and say:

" ' Alas! alas! thou great city,
   Thou mighty city, Babylon!
   In one hour has thy judgment come.

" ' Alas, alas, for the great city
   Where all who had ships at sea grew rich by her wealth!
   In one hour she has been laid waste!' "

And meanwhile in heaven a multitude is crying:

" 'Hallelujah! Salvation and glory and power belong to our God,
For his judgments are true and just.' "

Then at the end of the book there is John's dream of what
life on the earth shall be like when the Spirit of God controls it
all. In his vision John saw a great city coming down out of heaven
from God, the city of the new Jerusalem, with streets of gold
and walls that gleam like jewels. And through its gates the kings
of the earth come, bringing their glory into it. The city needs
no light of sun or moon to shine in it, said John, for the glory
of God enlightens it. Through its streets flows a river of life
from the throne of God, and on each side of the river grow the
trees of life, whose leaves are for the healing of the nations.

What his vision meant to John was that when life really begins
to be lived according to the spirit of Jesus, it will be more beautiful than even the greatest dream can show.

"Even so, come, Lord Jesus!" he prayed.

And then, as the last words in the Bible, it is written: "The
grace of the Lord Jesus Christ be with you all. Amen."

Index